Don't Look Back In Anger
The Black Monk of Pontefract

Books by Andy Evans

Displaced

When Spirits Break Free

The Division Bell

Don't Look Back in Anger
The Black Monk of Pontefract

Andy Evans

Poltergeist comes directly from the German word of the same spelling and entered the English dictionary in the 1850's. The term comes from the German word *Polter* meaning 'to make noise, knock, rattle' and *Geist* meaning 'ghost'

© 2015 Andy Evans. All rights reserved. No part of this book may be reproduced, stored in a retrieval system or transmitted in any form or by any means without the prior written permission of the author, except by a reviewer who may quote brief passages in a review to be printed by a newspaper, magazine or journal.
ISBN 978-1-326-26616-5

First Print

Acknowledgements

Thanks go out to everybody who made the book a reality.

Phil Bates and Mandy Welton - For guidance

Sasha Evans my daughter who entered the investigation with an open mind and never backed away from anything she could not explain.

Michelle Evans my long suffering wife who forgave me time and time again whenever I purchased another piece of equipment

Steve Hemingway without whom the journey would never have started.

Carol Fieldhouse who we first contacted and became a beacon and starting point for the research.

Glynn and Gill Gentry who were there from the start. Glynn was the rock and worked tirelessly to rationally explain anything we encountered.

Bil Bungay for his opener

Julie and Lee Shaw who joined us in the early days as independent witnesses

Glen Smith at Paratech UK Glen provides the best equipment available on today's market and I am proud to have used these during the investigation.

Sue Hughes for her patience when proof reading the impossible

Contents

Chapter 1   30 East Drive Chequerfield Pontefract

Chapter 2   Two Idiots and the Monk

Chapter 3   From Innocence to Reality

Chapter 4   Collecting the Evidence

Chapter 5   Stepping Into the Abyss

Chapter 6   Loading the Guns

Chapter 7   No Place Like Home

Chapter 8   Fact From Fiction

Chapter 9   When the Lights Go Out

Chapter 10 Next Steps Into the Abyss

Chapter 11 When the Lights Turned On

Chapter 12 Putting Fred to Bed

Introduction

The Black Monk of Pontefract
Kind permission of Bil Bungay film producer of When the Lights Went Out

In August 1966, Jean, Joe, Phillip (15) and Diane (12) Pritchard moved into 30 East Drive, Pontefract in West Yorkshire. Almost immediately, during the hot summer Bank Holiday, Phillip and his Grandmother first witnessed a baffling phenomenon. A fine layer of chalk-like dust falling not from the ceiling, but from a level below head height!!

In an effort to clean the dust up before Phillip's parents returned from holiday, Mrs Kelly (Phillip's Aunty who had been fetched to observe the falling dust) went to the kitchen for some cleaning implements, but as she went into the kitchen she slipped on a pool of water that had mysteriously appeared. Her efforts to mop up the water were thwarted by more pools of water appearing on the linoleum in front of her and Phillip's very eyes.

This was the beginning of several years of incredible, inexplicable events; green foam appearing from taps and the toilet, even after the water was turned off, the tea dispenser being activated, resulting in all the dried tea cascading onto the work surface, lights being turned off and on, plants leaping out of their pots and landing on the stairs, cupboards shaking violently, photographs being slashed with a sharp knife and an endless list of levitating and thrown objects – including a solid oak sideboard.

Dubbed 'Mr Nobody' by the local press in 1968, the family preferred to refer to the entity simply as 'Fred', perhaps it was their way of normalising 'It' as no number of initiatives could persuade whatever 'it' was, to leave the family in peace and house-proud mother Jean refused to be terrorised out of her house by an entity. Exorcisms were met with indignation; walls would seep water, faces were slapped, people were shoved down the stairs and Fred's hands would appear from nowhere and conduct the Christian songs aimed at shooing him off – whilst wearing huge women's fur gloves. In fact, many of Fred's antics were both amazing and often highly amusing, like when he calmly poured an entire jug of milk he removed from the fridge over a sceptical aunt, leaving the kids in stitches.

Ordinarily poltergeists (if this is what it was) aren't known for causing grievous bodily harm, and although Fred caused a few bruises and scrapes and lot of heart stopping scares, in particular to Diane – seemingly the focus of the haunting – it is rare for a poltergeist to become excessively violent and cause physical harm. But in the case of Fred, that indeed became the case. Late on in his residency, when both Phillip and Diane were beginning to exit adolescence, the activity reached a new climactic height with Diane's long hair suddenly standing on end, followed by her being dragged kicking and screaming up the stairs, an event that left her seriously traumatised and with clear, visible finger marks on her throat.

Today

Bil Bungay, Ad Man, Film Producer and new owner of the property reflects:

What possessed me (forgive the pun) to buy the most infamous haunted house in Europe? Simply because I had recently made a movie about the house called When the Lights Went Out with director and good friend of mine, and native of Pontefract, Pat Holden*.

After completing the movie, I was looking for original ways of promoting When The Lights Went Out when I discovered that the actual house, where all these incredible events allegedly happened, was for sale – and it was…er, cheap – so I bought it! This resulted in the coolest red carpet movie premier ever, where two competition winners walked the tiny red carpet down the garden path into Number 30 East Drive to watch the movie about that actual house.

Of course, the truth is that despite having visited a very dark house in Coventry and spoken with a family that were being terrorised by a poltergeist, I still remained stoically sceptical. To me, IF the Black Monk ever existed, then surely after 40 years, it would be long gone? An assumption that proved to be terrifyingly wrong.

During a gathering of the stars of the movie at the house, I met the neighbour Carol. She was quick to inform me that now the house was once again open to visitors – lots of visitors, the activity had started again in earnest – 'and by the way, Fred was stood by the stairs observing us'. Turned out that Carol was something of a psychic and had encountered the poltergeist a number of times in her adjoining property.

Needless to say, I was reluctant to regard her comments with anything less than the same healthy degree of scepticism I had carried around with me since I was first told the story by Pat some 20 years earlier. For me the idea of making a movie about a 'poltergeist that moved into a council house', instead of the clichéd creaking mansion house or dank medieval castle, was a sitter – I didn't feel I needed to believe in the existence of ghosts or poltergeists in order or justify making a movie about them. I mean – come on!

Then I met Hannah Clifford and Tasha Connor, the two starlets from my movie and suggested a photo as a memento. As we posed, a friend took a picture on my iPhone – and a phone with 75% charge went flat and died in a beat.

I tried not to think anything of that either, blaming a technical fault on a perfectly healthy iPhone, but I had to let the photo opportunity slip. Or so I had thought. After I had recharged my phone I checked to see if the picture was there, to no avail. In fact it wasn't until weeks later that the photograph suddenly appeared on the phone. I was fairly sure it hadn't been taken and I am certain it wasn't in my photo library immediately after I had recharged my phone, I checked thoroughly.

Then the stories started coming in from Carol the neighbour and now Key Holder of the house. Reports of 3-4am bumps and bangs coming from number 30, glowing blue balls of 'energy' in the corridor, the duvet on Carol's son's bed being formed into the shape of a man on his bed, the black shadow of a very tall entity coming through the wall into her house and so on. 'It' was back! Or rather the truth, it seemed, was that 'It' had always been there, living in quiet harmony with Jean Pritchard all the while, as in fact the activities had 'restarted' before I took possession of the property with the apparent sound of a TV blaring in Number 30, despite the property being completely empty; a report that had Philip Pritchard, now in his late 50's, understandably quite alarmed.

Then I witnessed something indisputable with my own eyes. A documentary about the house and local community was being made, and I took the opportunity to visit the production crew on their last day of filming. Being professionals they were fairly understated about any events that may have happened while they had filmed at the property; the kettle switching on and 'superheating' of its own volition, the case of the constantly missing thermostat (the remote kind that you sit on the mantelpiece), the researcher being pinned down onto the bed in the small room (might have been a night terror?) and my personal favourite – possible evidence of the poltergeist's continuing fascination with keys? Back in the Pritchard's day, a bunch of keys consisting of all the keys of the house fell from the chimney when Jean was brushing the flue (including a peculiar key said to be a large medieval door key) – so it was intriguing to me that a bunch of keys belonging to one of the producers had gone missing. The crew hunted high and low and had all but given up finding them when someone had the idea to look inside the old vacuum cleaner I had purchased from a charity shop to dress the house. To my knowledge, it doesn't work. And even if it did it would never have the power to suck up a heavy bunch of keys! Plus, I suspect you'd notice if you did. The crew hit the road at around 2am leaving me alone with two colleagues to tidy up. I went out into the garden to clear up any litter. Now what's interesting is that when you are in an environment like that – a place with a paranormal reputation – you find yourself being extra vigilant (and by now my spider senses were more than tingling). You think about every move you make. 'I am picking up this piece of litter, I am walking it to the wheelie bin, I am lifting the bin lid' and so on. So I remember clearly that it was a very cold and calm night, the streets were completely clear and I was definitely alone outside. I looked at the double gates and naturally wanted to secure them before my departure. One side of the wrought iron double gate was open, so I closed it, dropped the plunger into the hole and pushed, using a bit of effort, a concrete block against the gate securing it firmly. Nothing less than a determined individual was going to open that gate. And before you say it – there's no slope, no spring in the gate, no bush to hide a prankster in, nothing.

I turned back towards the house and decided it was time to get my colleagues out of the house for us to hit the road. They came racing out of the kitchen door (the only door I had the key for and therefore the only door open) and were understandably very relieved to finally get out. I'd lock the door and we'd be done. Except the keys had gone. No sign of them. But that wasn't the half of it. I glanced over at the back gate one last time and to my horror, the side I had closed 2 minutes earlier – plunger and all – was open again, and I mean completely open – 90 degrees, the concrete block simply pushed aside!

My first response (everyone does it) was to accuse my two colleagues of playing tricks on me, but I knew they had been upstairs installing a lampshade (in the dark!) the whole time. I definitely closed the gate and there was absolutely no one out at all. The hairs on the back of my neck took about an hour to settle back down.

It wasn't until the following day, when the locksmith was replacing the lock, that Carol my psychic neighbour casually explained to me that it 'happened all the time'. 'It' or 'Fred', as by now I too had started to call him out of some form of respect (in the vain hope that he would spare me), moved around the neighbourhood, this was confirmed by other neighbours that have subsequently complained to me personally about the entity running passed their windows after hours… as if I could somehow stop 'Fred' from freaking out the locals!!

Friends have since had the courage to stay overnight, smart, grounded, healthily sceptical friends. The list of things that occurred to them boggle the mind, subtle stuff, but nevertheless real.

Other visitors described columns of ice-cold air in the corridor, every radiator in the house being turned up full (reported by a friend that installs radiators, he had turned them all down himself and was bemused by what had turned them all full on by the morning) and the cupboard under the stairs being impossible to open – trust me, it opens easily…

Only one group of friends seemingly had nothing happen to them, but I had observed how calm the house felt when they went for their visit. Plus they did reach for the beers (perfectly understandable!) and it is recognised that stimulants are not advised if you want to experience something paranormal – don't ask me why, but a lot of the stuff can be quite subtle, and a few bevies have been known to take the edge of things! That said, when we walked in, Darren, from next door, was trying to put a hundred pieces of puzzle, that had been spread all over the carpet, back into their box – except the box was thoroughly taped up, as it had been since I bought it from the charity shop. He broke the side of the box in my presence to return the pieces.

Chapter One
30 East Drive Pontefract

The Poltergeist of Pontefract. Now this was a tale told countless times within the darkened confines of the schoolyard.

The early 1970's were a bustling, busy and prosperous time for the mining towns and villages of West Yorkshire. Coal was the king who reigned aloft and supreme amidst the sprawling pits and council estates of his kingdom. Daytime was spent at school for the miners' children and the darkening early evening hours were spent simply 'playing out'.

Kick out Can, Hide and Seek, Kerby and Kiss Catch were to name just a few of the games we would play with nothing in the way of technology, planning or expense.

Just before 'calling in time' when our mothers would shout our names through open windows, we always delved into childish stories of ghostly tales of local hauntings.

Featherstone, like many mining communities, was still deeply embroiled in its Victorian beginnings. Dimly lit terraces of back to back housing, interlaced with alley ways, added to the atmosphere to fuel any tale of ghastly terror. The arrival of VHS players brought about an influx of movies focused on paranormal stories from across the globe, the most famous one being the story of an American girl being possessed by the devil himself. It was rumoured that when the film was shown for the first time viewers were given a 'sick bag' on entry to the cinema. The film for its time truly was a shocker, however, looking back I suspect this could merely have been a marketing exercise adding to the shock factor to feed the ever-growing worldwide audiences of thrill seekers.

Despite VHS being a very portable gateway of terror and fright we had our very own real and well documented horror happening, almost on our own doorstep.

According to headlines in the local press a monk from the medieval times was terrorizing a family who had moved into a council house in the nearby town of Pontefract.

The town has its roots deeply embedded in the annals of history. It was the site of a Cluniac Priory founded in 1090 by Robert de Lacy dedicated to Saint John the Evangelist. The priory was dissolved by royal authority in 1539.

From 1648 to 1649 Pontefract Castle was laid under siege by Oliver Cromwell who said it was '... one of the strongest inland garrisons in the kingdom.'

Three sieges by the Parliamentarians left the town 'impoverished and depopulated'. In March 1649, after the third siege, the Pontefract inhabitants, fearing a fourth, petitioned Parliament for the castle to be demolished. In their view, the castle was a magnet for trouble, and in April 1649 demolition began. (The ruins of the castle still remain today and are publicly accessible.)

Given its history, it was likely that Pontefract could be the site of hauntings, however the disturbance making the headlines did not arise from any of the historic places you would imagine. The castle's ramparts and site of the priory remained silent and it was a local Council house which seemed to be the focus of paranormal activity.

The tenants, it seemed, had awoken a monk from his centuries of slumber and it was said he now focused his unwanted attentions on the family's daughter. From what I remember the activity ceased and over time, other, more up to date stories took centre stage of back yard gossip and local infamy.

Gradually even my own memory fogged over. I remembered the vague details of the haunting but believed the house had been demolished leaving simply an empty space of grassland where the property once stood.

In 2012 I was surprised when the story, from my lost youth, once again made headline news. A film company released a movie about the haunting and the monk again became the focus of both local and national interest.

Despite the movie being filmed at a different location, the local press gave out the actual address of the property, which still survived, contrary to my belief that it had been demolished.

The movie reignited my interest in the story and like countless others my wife Michelle and I paid our hard earned money and visited the local cinema. Always one to impress, I immediately drove Michelle to the address of the house. Admittedly we were both amused to find a large group of thrill seekers stood outside the semi-detached property probably hoping to catch a glimpse of the spirit inside.

Despite our own amusement at the gathering crowd I realised that we, too, had been drawn back to the story which had given us a glimpse into something we truly did not understand. However, this resurrected interest in the story, faded and was put on the back burner mainly due to my wife, Michelle, being diagnosed with a rare neurological condition. I was almost half way to completing my fifth book but caring for Michelle and work commitments curtailed this. My interest, however, in this particular haunting continued and in May 2014 I offered to show my friend Steve the location of the property in question.

I had met Steve some twelve months earlier through work connections. As our working partnership grew it became apparent that we shared an interest in art, literature and the paranormal.

Our first joint visit to 30 East Drive had no pre-planning and we simply travelled to visually take in the location of the house. It was mid-May and a mini heat wave had taken everyone by surprise. On arrival the house appeared like all the others on the sprawling council estate, known as Chequerfield. It stood on a corner, semi-detached with an area of grassland and small trees immediately in front. In the mid-day sun the house and surroundings looked far from imposing and anyone, not knowing its history, would never have given it a second glance.

It was early Sunday afternoon and the street was empty of people who, most likely, were busy sunning themselves in backyards with barbeques warming and children splashing about in hastily inflated paddling pools.

Despite being empty for a number of years the house blended into its surroundings. The privet hedges were neatly cut, the garden tended and vertical blinds and curtains were neatly drawn.

Our intentions on that day were simply to look at the house from the road outside but before long a mature lady appeared carrying a shopping bag advertising a local convenience shop. We said hello and asked if she knew anything of the story of the house. Despite her heavy shopping she took the time to tell us her own opinion. It transpired that she had lived on the estate for most of her life and told us the whole story had been fabricated by the family's daughter, who desperately sought attention.

Although this being a negative response it was an honest one. In our opinion the film had over dramatized the true events and as writers we wanted the 'nitty gritty' of what actually was the truth.

Having seen the house close up we were ready to leave and head back home when another woman emerged from a nearby car which had parked immediately in front of us.

Careful not to startle the newcomer, who stepped onto the pavement, we exchanged the customary and polite greetings, still held in esteem amongst the northern working classes, with her. Once these pleasantries had been exchanged, we were surprised at the friendly response given when we asked the lady if she knew anything about the house and the stories about it.

The questions seemed to excite and invigorate her and she introduced herself as 'Carol' and explained she was the key holder to the property.

Instantly I felt a rush of adrenalin and catching Steve's eye I knew he felt the same. If thoughts could be heard a joint shout of 'Bingo' would, I am sure, have resounded across the street disturbing the quiet of the nearby houses.

Enthusiasm seemed to pour from Carol in never ending waves as she quickly explained her role as the key holder and general caretaker of the property. With hindsight, I should have taken a Dictaphone, but with no forward planning, and as we had merely gone to take in the atmosphere of the property and its communal surroundings, I had only a camera with me.

My foggy recollections, from youth, had attached themselves to the story of the original hauntings of the early 1970's. As usual, however, memory plays tricks on us over time and I was still surprised that the house had not been demolished or decayed over the years following the headlines. But the house had continued, despite the reported horrors and the family, seemingly targeted by a dark spirit, had continued living in their home.

A second mental shout of bingo, or rather, a yelp of trepidation came when Carol produced a set of keys from her handbag.

'Do you want to look inside?' For me this seemed simply more than an offer of generosity. She, more than anyone, knew about the house and its history and it felt like a gauntlet had been thrown.

Both Steve and I originate from working class backgrounds and the challenge was readily, if foolishly, accepted. Perhaps, momentarily, time stood still totally in keeping with the haunting, or the realization that we were about to cross the threshold of the house. But now we were just an arm's length away from the white UPVC door to, who knew what? If there was a dark force inside we stood on the brink of finding out just what was inside the bricks and mortar interior. (With all the best intentions when we set out on the journey of writing about true hauntings it was at this very moment I admitted to myself that I had never expected to play a leading role in the unknown, but before a fake coughing fit or an imaginary text to say I was needed at home could be conjured up the key was in the lock and the door opened.)

'It's only me Fred,' Carol called through the door.

'Thank you', was my initial thought, the house was in fact occupied after all.

'Who's Fred?' I asked with a slight hesitance in my voice.

'Fred's the nickname we have given to the Monk,' Carol calmly replied and she pushed open the door.

The door opened silently. There was no creaking, reminiscent of an ancient drawbridge or the breaking of a seal to some long gone ancient tomb. The PVC door and the threshold of the house was as ordinary as that of yours or mine.

Two doors to our right were immediately explained as being a toilet and the coal 'house'. Momentarily I felt a shiver as I remembered that it was supposed to be the coal house which had been active in the original hauntings stories. Coal house is a northern term for the brick built adjoining building which, each month, the coal miners would receive their ton of coal as part of their working rights.

As the second door was opened I immediately felt a wave of disappointment crashing into me. The Pontefract Poltergeist had been covered by both local and international news and the view from the open doorway was not as I expected. It wasn't a dark, musty place with malevolent forces, obvious to anybody that I would have described if I was writing a 'creepy' book. The kitchen before me was just normal. Despite the windows being covered by beige coloured, vertical blinds the room was light. Oak cupboard doors on conventional kitchen units with walls in keeping with the modern style fire surround of polished wood and marble extract.

Beyond the fireplace was a 1970's style laminate table and four chairs. To the left a battered looking replica leather armchair which must have been a prototype to the recliners marketed today.

This, to me was not what I had ever expected to see. A standard council house, in daylight and with the distant sounds of kids enjoying the warm weather. This was not the kind of place you would have associated with a haunting or perhaps I have watched too many movies?

'He's around,' Carol announced breaking the silence and our somewhat bemused thoughts.

Carol pointed to a book which lay innocently on the Formica breakfast bar which ran at a 90 degree angle from the wall, almost dividing the one room into two.

'That wasn't there yesterday,' she said, as if this was just an everyday occurrence within the house.

'That's his party piece,' she continued pointing to the four chairs which had been pulled out from beneath the wooden table as if invisible guests remained seated waiting for breakfast, which was never to come.

The book was iconic to say the least. A black covered hardback of the bible. Without hesitation I took a photograph and immediately felt content that I had captured an image from the house. Two more amateurish shots were taken of the dining table arrangement before Carol eased the chairs back underneath the table and unlocked the double French style doors into the living room.

Before we could take in the ambience of the room, we were startled by the dull sound of a key turning in a lock behind us. Both glass panelled doors were closed and Carol held a small key tightly in the grasp of her right hand.

'Don't worry,' she explained, 'the family believed in locking the spirit within rooms they were not in.'

A little uncomfortable with this fact we focused our attention on the living room which was in keeping with the kitchen. There were no dark corners, no cobwebs or obvious portals between the spirit and living world. The room was clean, free from dust and seemed homely, if not a little outdated with the choice of furniture and décor. Everything within the house we would later learn had been added by the film company, leaving only remnants of the original fittings as being truly authentic at the time of the original publicised haunting.

It was still odd, however, that the double glazed panelled doors separating the kitchen and living room were locked behind us. Our host briefly explained this was in keeping with routine. The family, at the time of the alleged hauntings, had attempted to keep the poltergeist at bay whenever they were in the kitchen. Foolhardy or simple innocence of what they could not understand, sprang immediately to mind. If a spirit could enter and leave a dimension unseen by the human eye then surely a simple lock and key could never alter or stop its free passage.

The fake leather settee had seen better days and looked tired even within the outdated décor it dominated. The fake stone fireplace fitted nicely into the scene and was similar to the one I remembered from my own childhood. A glass framed china cabinet immediately to the side of the door leading to the stairs appeared neglected and was now filled only with a mishmash of cheap and tasteless objects which only added to the emptiness which now seemed to be filling the atmosphere of the house.

Beyond the next door was the staircase. Two mirrors adorned adjacent walls and a cheaply framed print of King Richard took centre stage on the main wall.

The carpeted staircase was quite steep and narrow in keeping with the council layouts of the time. Perhaps in the 1950's post war boom architects had summarized that if the working man took less time to go upstairs to sleep, he would take less time to wake, return downstairs, and work again.

Nothing in the upstairs rooms filled us with dread or excitement. Three bedrooms and a small bathroom with no hint of malice or foreboding evident in the light of day. The smallest of the bedrooms had once been the room of the daughter at the time of the alleged hauntings. Interestingly the polystyrene ceiling tiles, popular in the 1970's and now probably banned as a fire hazard were heavily marked with dints and gouge marks. I speculated that these could have been scars of poltergeist activity as objects were thrown or they could have just been the result of clumsy workmanship or just time. Speculation and personal opinion have to be discredited and for us the source of the marks would remain unanswered, adding only to the mystery surrounding the house.

Pausing at the top of the stairs it soon became apparent our host was not at her best. Her movements became laboured and she held onto the heavily glossed wooden stair banister which was horizontal before the descent downstairs.

'He's here,' she announced in a hushed whisper, 'he always makes me feel like this.'

Despite her apparent unease, our boyish excitement took over and looking back we selfishly became more interested in what might appear than the health of the poor woman accompanying us.

I quickly took random shots of the staircase and views of the bedrooms from where we stood. Nothing in the view finder gave me reason for jubilation and after six or seven snaps I turned the camera off.

No sooner had I stopped taking pictures than our host seemed to recover and she warned us to take hold of the wooden rail to our right as we descended the steep stairs.

'Fred has a habit of giving visitors a little push,' Carol announced as she led the way. Like two school boys terrified of heights we both held onto that wooden anchor as if there was no tomorrow. Other visitors to the house may record the obvious finger marks along the wooden banister rail as being paranormal. If however finger prints were to be taken then I guess the guilty parties would point only to us.

Back downstairs and in the living room internal confidence rose within me and I asked about the story of the monk who was said to haunt the house.

From what I had read and heard from local folklore the story had centred on a monk from the local priory. Paedophilia unfortunately was not just a modern problem and one monk in particular had crossed the line of what could never be accepted. His liking for young girls had got the better of his dark inner desires and unfortunately he had raped and killed a local girl. Thankfully, even in the past laws of time, this was unacceptable and the monster was captured and hanged.

Carol immediately corrected me on my historical facts. The monk who was supposed to haunt the house had been innocent.

'Fred,' she began to explain, 'Or Father Michael, to use his proper name...' The sentence was cut short as four heavy footsteps were clearly heard from the room above our heads. The noise startled and confused both Steve and I. We distinctly heard four heavy footsteps on wood, this despite us knowing all the first floor rooms were carpeted and none of them had bare boards flooring.

Our host however continued as if the noise was of no significance and was in fact ordinary.

Father Michael was a twin and it had been the other brother who carried out the murder. For some reason the murderous twin had been wearing his brothers ring and it was this which the locals had found near to the dead girl's naked body. Unfortunately brotherly love was too much for the innocent Father Michael and so a man, free from sin, was led to the town's gallows. No records exist, unfortunately, of the guilty brother's continued existence or the circumstances of his eventual demise.

Father Michael had been hanged for his brother's crime and his still struggling body was cut from the rope and pushed down a nearby well. Maybe it had been the spectators guilty conscious of seeing a man of the cloth take his last condemned breath on the rope, or they were simply bored of the longevity of the hanging and cut the procedure short before he was dead. Either way, poor Michael was said to have been thrown into the well, out of sight and hopefully out of mind.

Unfortunately we have yet to find accurate records to determine whether or not Pontefract's public gallows were once situated in front of the house as the story of the Black Monk suggests. The position of the house is perhaps less than half a mile from the once impregnable castle and elevated above the surrounding land.

If you wanted to draw in crowds before the modern day of stadium then perhaps this could have been the ideal location. The story of the well, however, could be a different matter. Council workmen had recorded seeing a capping stone situated between the house and the adjoining property. Old wells, either polluted or no longer in use were often sealed. Could this be the final resting place of the monk?

Satisfied we had seen everything there was to see we returned to the kitchen, the doors being unlocked so we could enter. The afternoon sunlight continued breaking through the blind of the shaded window and the room remained light and free from any oppression you might imagine in a so called haunted location.

The chairs, however, had moved. Despite both of us witnessing Carol push all four of the seats back beneath the table, all four were now obviously pulled away as if waiting for guests to be seated. Adding more to the mystery the bible had also moved from its original position. Digital cameras thankfully offer us the basics of modern photography without the need for expertise. Dark rooms and never ending waiting for family snaps are thankfully now replaced with instant playback. In minutes the digital world reinforced what we suspected. The bible had moved. Not just a small movement but about sixty centimetres across the kitchen work surface and angled in a different position. Chairs previously observed being neatly placed beneath the table, by Carol, were once again pulled back, space on each for someone to be seated on.

We now had our first two pieces of evidence to work with. A bible which had been moved and four chairs seemingly altered in position, from when we last viewed them, in a locked room!

Outside, the dappled rays of sunshine, made our experience surreal and it seemed we had momentarily entered a place very different to a world we understood. People, busy with their own day to day routines cheerfully passed by enjoying the early warmth the sun offered. We entered the house with open minds sitting on an invisible fence with belief and disbelief balanced evenly. In a short space of time, the equilibrium had shifted and intrigue joined the balance.

Better was to come later as I transferred the captured images from the digital camera to my laptop. Most of the photographs showed an ordinary house, dated in its appearance but seemingly tranquil in the early summer's rays.

Chatting at the top of the stairs I had innocently taken five pictures of the staircase. Nothing seemed unusual and the images were to be for my own records only. After all I had been within the four walls of the most famous house in Yorkshire, if not Europe, as it had been quoted.

Each image mattered and every opportunity was captured on camera. The first three snapshots showed a well-lit staircase, sunlight cascading onto the hall from the glazed door immediately to the left of the hallway as it meets the steep staircase. The fourth was different. The ambient sunshine was no more. On the staircase a black mist had formed which seemed to have ascended from the third and fourth step. Close up examination appears to show the shape having a body mass dressed in a dark robe and head cowl.

Photograph five, taken seconds later reverts back to sunlight and serenity.

Had we momentarily captured the infamous Black Monk of Pontefract or were we simply being misguided by simple tricks of light? Here now was the basis of our first investigation.

Carol, I suspect, may have misjudged our determination to finally uncover the true secret of 30

East Drive. Since the film had been released there was a steady stream of thrill seekers wishing to be part of the Black Monk experience and she was inundated with visitors wishing to witness happenings. I think, she thought, we were simply part of this procession of people and that our interest would soon diminish as our initial excitement subsided.

Perhaps this was the reason she reluctantly agreed to a return visit for us, an overnight stay without the comfort daylight hours offered. In the dark atmosphere of night time, maybe she suspected this would be the last she would hear from us.

Chapter Two
Two Idiots and a Monk

With bravado rapidly diminishing we were set for our first overnight stay at the house. The Black Monk had filled my teenage years with trepidation and horror. Fears from further afield had added to my dread of the unknown and films such as The Exorcist, Amityville Horror and more lately Nightmare on Elm Street were still deeply embedded within my memory.

Horror on the television screen fascinates many but it is a fright which can easily be switched off at the click of a switch. Reality is quite different and as we neared the house our nerves kicked into overdrive. Being from a council estate very much like the one at Chequerfield I should have felt at ease with my surroundings but as we drew closer I felt a tightness gripping me from inside and feelings of panic began to crash into me like an unstoppable tide of dread. Childhood stories rose again within me and I fought a desperate battle between adolescent story and middle age rationale.

Perhaps the idea of the book had been born under false bravado. Two men exchanging ghost stories under the safety of familiar surroundings and daylight hours were now gone and it was time to face either reality or fiction.

Despite being almost eight o'clock in the evening when we reached No 30, the temperature was still peaking at 20 degrees Celsius. Summer was in full throe and the semi- detached house of red brick was bathed in brilliant sunshine. Neatly trimmed hedges of healthy privet and tendered gardens gave the suggestion of occupation to any passer-by ignorant to the story and history of the house.

There was no going back. We had set our sights on a full overnight stay and whatever the outcome we would honour what we had foolishly set out to do.

Looking back now with hindsight and experience we were completely naïve and under equipped for what we intended. Armed with just a torch, camcorder and mobile phones to record our findings we had entered into something neither of us could comprehend.

Colin Wilson had investigated the haunting thirty five years ago and included his findings in his own book simply titled Poltergeist. His own research had been extensive and supported by first hand testimonies from the Pritchard family, family members and neighbours. Our own investigation was merely based on curiosity and naivety.

As initial nervousness gradually subsided we took stock of our surroundings. The house seemed the same as it had done on our first visit, except this time we were alone.

Nothing seemed out of place as we inspected each room in turn and the only change in the interior environment of the house was that of disappointment.

The recent film had portrayed a violent entity capable of dragging a teenager upstairs by her throat, smashing furniture and offering a full blown visual manifestation. Instead a picture of dreary sadness filled each and every room. Tired furniture and ornamental fixtures, none of which were true to the house or story now attempted to give a feeling to an age long since gone. On selling the property five years before the Pritchard's had left little of their existence there and the purchasing film producer had filled the property with furnishings from local charity shops in an attempt to recreate the early 1970's.

The wooden single bed in what would have been Diane's room remained broken as it had done on our first visit. Legs beneath the headboard snapped away leaving the footboard rising as if some ocean liner was making its final descent beneath the waves. If the haunting was so violent why then had nothing changed?

As darkness fell we settled ourselves in the main bedroom which would have been Joe and Jean's private space.

All houses, old or new, have their own audible noises due to changes in temperature so it was not too unusual for us to hear slight bangs and creaks within the famous walls. Soon, however, we began to wonder if what we were hearing was just normal? On trepid investigation, noises heard downstairs were duplicated each and every time we moved position between the two floors. It soon became almost like a cat and mouse game. Whichever room we were in audible noises could be heard elsewhere. Temperatures within the four walls were quite normal for early summer and in no room were we met with cold spots or chills. This was a disappointment. In all the television shows I had seen, regarding paranormal investigation, there was always a cold spot whenever a manifestation was about to appear. 30 East Drive was the opposite with a feeling of warmth slowly subsiding with the sinking of the sun.

The bedroom was also a disappointment. It was here, almost forty years ago, that a pair of fur gloves had allegedly appeared and clapped along to Onward Christian Soldiers, being recited in horror by a family member of the Pritchard's whom it was said witnessed the phenomena. But for us there was no gloves, no habit clad spectres and no sign of anything unusual at all. Fortunately we were still pumped up with the adrenalin purely from being inside this famous house, so we moved onto the smaller bedroom with expectations still high. Nothing seemed out of place and we soon turned and left it to go to the third bedroom which had been Philip Pritchard's.

Immediately we knew that this particular room was different. The air felt heavy, oppressive and stifling. On visual inspection there was nothing in the room to offer any reason for these feelings of dread. Carpeted and furnished with a larger than single bed, albeit without sheets or pillows, all should have been in keeping with the rest of the house. Despite the jokes and banter both Steve and I both commented on feelings of headache and nausea. The air around us felt weighted with unseen energy and it was not long before we retreated back onto the narrow landing. Was this the encroachment of paranormal entities entering the realm of the living? Was this simply the effects of a house, tightly secured with double glazing with very little opportunity for fresh air to welcome visitors? Whatever the reason we felt uncomfortable and took respite on the bed in the main bedroom.

As the night closed in, the interior of the house seemed to change. Shadows grew and beckoned as if they, too, were part of the mystery which for generations had surrounded the house.

Thankfully neither of us scares easily. Steve having spent many years working in the psychiatric hospitals of South Yorkshire and myself working the rich coal seams underground as a miner. To expect the unexpected was already ingrained within us from our everyday working lives.

The first of the noises started. Heavy, dulcet knockings, in sequences of three, coming from downstairs. Everyone knows that houses settle with rising and dropping atmospheric conditions and timber and steel expands and contracts with temperature but these were not those sounds. These were very different. The house had been empty for several years and the heating system was defunct. The noises we were hearing could not be credited to copper pipes of cooling water and seemed to change location depending on where we were at any given time.

From downstairs footsteps could clearly be heard from the room above, just as on our first visit, heavy footsteps walking across a wooden floor. Apart from the bathroom and kitchen every room within the house was still carpeted. Cautiously we made our way upstairs ever careful to hold onto the heavily glossed white handrail running along the staircase, mindful of the story of The Black Monk having allegedly dragged the daughter of the family by the throat up these very stairs in the hauntings of 1974. A Grandmother clock, taking pride of place at the top of the staircase, had also supposedly been smashed to pieces due to an unseen force hurtling it down the stairs to its final sad resting place on the downstairs hallway. 'Fred' it seemed had a temper to be reckoned with. I felt somewhat disappointed when told he sometimes gave visitors a push if they walk the staircase without a firm grip on the rail because being a Yorkshire man I would have preferred a proper 'shove' rather than a push. Disappointment ebbed into me as I took the final step. No invisible hands had pressed against me and I was not lying in a broken heap at the foot of the staircase. I had reached the upstairs landing safely and feelings of disappointment bore into me and despite the footsteps heard earlier, everything now lay silent.

We cautiously checked every room, in the hope something had been moved or been displaced from its original position. Nothing seemed out of place despite the footsteps and no fluctuations in temperature were obvious. Just as feelings of disappointment began to take hold, sporadic bangs and knocks started coming from one the rooms downstairs. Despite rising adrenalin we stood fast and listened, with not a small amount of trepidation. Again, it was obvious the noises were nothing like those of a house structure settling, more those I would have attributed to the sounds of intruders taking idiotic advantage of a vacant property. It crossed my mind that perhaps a burglar would offer us less of a threat if we were to openly confront him, as a thief is usually of human form, after all. The Black Monk of Pontefract however, if all accounts were to be believed, was a force to be reckoned with and held significant power and strength, not of this world.

The sounds continued throughout the evening and into the early hours. It seemed we were in a game of cat and mouse. When we were upstairs, the banging noises were downstairs; when we were in the living room or kitchen the bangs appeared to resound upstairs.

Looking back it was quite comical and I now think back to the closing scenes of a Benny Hill show. Each episode always ended with a chase, albeit speeded up, but with the pursuer never actually catching the prey.

As dawn broke it was obvious we had experienced something we could not fully explain. There is an old saying which refers to 'being led a merry dance.' For us we felt that during those overnight hours at East Drive, we had been led just that. We had no tangible evidence the house had been, or indeed remained haunted. History and time blurs true recollection and authenticity, that's how legends are created, fact, or just a story, being enhanced as it is re-told.

The late 60's and early 70's were a time of film producers selling supernatural tales to a growing worldwide audience. Frankenstein had sadly lost his appeal to the younger generation in the new age of science and technology as, in theory, the story became more plausible. Tales of demonic poltergeists now attracted the thrill seekers and adrenalin junkies. However did those same innocent viewers realise there could, in fact, be some truth behind the stories they now sat and watched whilst eating their popcorn and ice cream?

Despite fatigue, excitement still prevailed. Locking the front door behind us, blackbirds and other birds singing a merry morning chorus of their own to welcome a new day, could be heard.

East Drive for the moment had offered little. We felt we were simply been given morsels of what the house could offer and we were hungry for more. No demonic black force or crazed monk desperate for revenge had materialized and the house, renowned nationally for its ferocity in the realms of supernatural phenomena had been pretty tame. We had, without doubt, experienced things that we could not easily offer rational explanations for, however sometimes imagination can be both powerful, deceptive and cruel.

The written chapters which follow are not and were never meant to be a work of fiction. They are not designed to scare audiences or snare innocents into believing in the paranormal for my own personal gain.

I know scare tactics sell to a never ending audience of want-to-be believers and sceptics alike. The unexplainable has an attraction all of its own.

Steve and I, at this point were simply intrigued, sceptical and totally open to the story of the Black Monk of Pontefract. This supposedly dark robed figure of the 1970's had failed to move any furniture during the night.

No ornaments lay shattered on any carpeted floor and neither of us had been put in fear for our lives after being dragged up the stairs by our throats. However, despite the lack of drama we both agreed, something was amiss at the property. East Drive was just one of six local properties we had originally set out to naively investigate and record as bystanders to possible paranormal activity. However, with just that one overnight stay we had become ensnared. Something made this location very different and from then on we focused all investigations on this house alone.

Within a few days we were already planning our next visit to the house. Technology had let us down for recording any phenomena present during our twelve hour overnight stay. Our weaponry of choice had consisted of Steve's up to date Samsung mobile telephone, albeit with decent camera capability and my own Korean, of no known branded name, digital camera. We had also had a big gun in our arsenal. We had managed to borrow a decent camcorder with basic night vision capabilities. Unfortunately, the two idiot's now taking charge of this up to date piece of equipment somehow had pressed the wrong button. Video footage was blank, hours wasted with nothing to show. We were on a sharp learning curve and at this point this curve seemed to be pointing downwards.

It was obvious in the days following we really did need to accustom ourselves to the world of paranormal investigation. Unexplained phenomena unless accurately recorded and scrutinized remains open to sceptics. Without proof, our own experiences would be torn apart by anybody wishing to dismiss whatever science had already confirmed and documented. Personal accounts would never hold up to scrutiny and we soon realised if the book was to hold any credence we would have to offer the reader concrete tangible evidence.

Before our next visit we would have to invest financially in reliable equipment. For us this went against the grain of what we originally had set out to do, which was to visit a supposed haunted location and leave with our own thoughts and may be share them with others. Our overnight visit to East Drive put a stop to any thoughts of a brief encounter. We were now in it for the long haul and we believed that infinite proof was paramount to every move we were now to make, if that was possible.

Chapter Three
From Innocence to Reality

Colin Wilson in his own book 'Poltergeist' had given hints that the phenomena he recorded from first-hand accounts of the Pritchard family, six years after the original activity had ceased, were the result of poltergeist activity. Unfortunately, Colin Wilson may have been misled. Some of his research focused on the findings of a local historian who claimed to have found records of a Cluniac monk being hanged for the rape and murder of a young girl. Pontefract, with its Castle and nearby priories fitted neatly into what the family experienced. As my own interest in the story took hold I re-opened the case and can find no records of a monk being hanged for any offence at Pontefract. If one of the priories had carried out justice on such a scale I feel this would have been done within closed walls. Paedophilia, if not a recognised word back then, would certainly have occurred, even taking account of the much lower marriage age of the day. I doubt however any religious organization would publicise any such wrong doing by one of their order and carry out a public execution on a hill visible for miles around.

This bothered me for weeks to come. If records had been available back in the 1970's why then were they no longer open to scrutiny in the age of the World Wide Web. From where had the historian drawn his information? Why had this been accepted without further investigation? Had the Black Monk of Pontefract simply been born out of misguided information fuelled by local history surrounding the nearby castle and priories or was there more to the story crudely left undone for forty years?

The Pritchard family insisted a dark robed figure inhabited the house and was responsible for the violent paranormal activity plaguing their everyday lives. The mould was cast and the monk reigned supreme. Local newspapers and television newsreel had revelled in the supernatural tale unfolding on their doorstep.

Chequerfield was now on the map. One single semi-detached council property had raised the curtain of fame. The Black Monk was now a celebrity and countless stories would unfold about the ferocity of the haunting. Furniture being smashed and a grandmother clock thrown down the stairs had been documented. Eggs frying mysteriously on the cold kitchen floor and showers of fine dust appearing from nowhere only to settle on the carpeted floors were neither rational nor normal.

Why then had nothing sinister occurred during our overnight vigil? Was the whole story a hoax generated by the Pritchard children to gain attention? Had the perpetrator simply faded and diminished or were we simply being tested and played with? For me this was now a question I had to uncover. In my book Displaced I spent twenty years searching for the truth. East Drive now became my next target.

Technology is one word most of us over 40 duck our heads down and avoid. Unfortunately Steve and I fall into this category and we were now on a back footing. We knew little of equipment used in paranormal investigations and the next few days were spent online researching. Funds were limited and options for purchasing everything needed could never be an option open to us. Instead we needed to prioritize and the first choice was an electromagnetic field meter.

There is a widespread belief among paranormal researchers that entities emit an electromagnetic field and their presence can be detected by EMF meters. They suggest that ghosts disturb the existing background (geo) magnetic field whenever they are present.

EMF meters detect fields emitted by moving electrically charged objects. Electromagnetic field theory lies at the combination of an electric field, produced by a charged object, and the magnetic field created when the charged object moves. For us this would be our starting point. We were possibly dealing with something we could not see. A device which could possibly visually alert us to an unexplained presence would be invaluable in the research for the book. Not a fan of online shopping I again wasted time searching for local stores stocking the equipment. None could be found so, reluctantly I turned to EBay and ordered the one with the best customer reviews. Within a few days the package arrived. Thankfully operating instructions were simple with just a single on off switch and a series of lights from green to red. Green indicated no readings and red gave evidence of high readings.

Thankfully the colour green remained consistent in every room of my own home. If the equipment was reliable this meant no spirits had followed me from East Drive.

The countdown to our next overnight stay reached lift off and again my heart raced as the glass panelled door opened giving us access to allegedly one of the most haunted house in Europe. The EMF meter held pride of place amongst the digital cameras but this was not our only new tool to uncover the truth. Glynn had now become the third idiot to join us. A lifelong friend to my family, Glynn had over thirty years of experience of mixing with paranormal phenomena. Unlike the newly acquired EMF meter Glynn does not run on batteries and can always be relied upon to give an honest explanation of any experiences we were to encounter.

With trepidation we again cautiously checked each and every room for anything out of the ordinary. There was nothing, but it was obvious that we had not been the only earth bound visitors since our last overnight stay. In the coal house was a piece of paper with three pennies positioned within drawn circles around them. The middle penny lay slightly out of its circle but this meant nothing. We had not personally placed this trigger object and any movement could have been caused by any rational explanation including human interference.

The same trigger objects were found in the living room, bathroom and main bedroom. All of these coins remained undisturbed. I was uncertain if these 'traps' would in fact act as being reliable evidence at all. I simply could not imagine a powerful force from the spirit world would carefully take time to push a coin out of its corresponding drawn circle. Surely the infamous Black Monk would simply scatter the offered objects with ferocity and disdain as a warning to whoever visited?

The EMF meter gave no readings in any of the rooms and only when tested near to live electrical sockets did it prove to be working. The LED lights grew quickly from green to red, indicating high readings.

With every room checked we settled ourselves into the main bedroom of the house. Colin Wilson in his book 'Poltergeist' had taken statements from the family that a pair of fur gloves had appeared around the door in the early hours.

Frightened by what was happening, it was reported the family prayed and sang the popular hymn 'Onward Christian Soldiers' in the hope Christianity would send whatever it was, back into the darkness from which it came. The song it seemed had little effect and the gloves (a pair owned by the grandmother of the family) clapped in tune with the song sung out by the frightened family.

Tonight however the room felt welcoming and safe. There were mirror fronted wardrobes along the inner wall facing the windows and a double bed, without sheets or pillows which offered some comfort, against the wall. The only thing out of character was the cheap, veneered dressing table which was obviously a period piece added for authenticity.

The EMF meter continued to give us nothing. The same deadline readings from my own home were reflected in each room of East Drive. With hope fading we were suddenly given a timely lift. A small paperback bible on the crude dressing table gave high readings from the meter. The oval mirror on the table gave out duplicate readings but whenever the apparatus was moved away the readings became negative.

Nothing else within the room registered and questions surfaced. The movie 'The Lights Went Out' captivated audiences across UK cinemas and it was now the film producer who owned the house. Was the house wired to sell the film? Hidden speakers could be covertly placed to produce footsteps and banging phenomena. Electrical discharge is also simple to produce by anyone with just a basic knowledge of home electronics.

Readings on the mirror and bible continued. The following two hours we searched everywhere for hidden wires, microphones, speakers and anything which could be used for deception. Suspicions rose and we decided to lift the mirror from its position and check the object thoroughly for anything which could create a magnetic field. Carefully the mirror was dismantled and rebuilt. Nothing had been tampered with and our suspicions dwindled.

What would prove interesting when we later played back the audio recording is that when we moved the mirror a heavy growl can clearly be heard lasting for several seconds.

The house was clean. Any noise or variant in electrical field in our opinion was not the work of a technician to fool visitors and keep the story of the Black Monk alive.

Eventually the readings subsided and did not return during the rest of the night. Surprisingly no unexplained phenomena were recorded in the smallest bedroom. Given the story of the original haunting this surprised us. The room had belonged to Diane Pritchard, youngest of the two children. The story gave suggestion it was the daughter who had in fact generated the poltergeist activity. If this were the case why then was her bedroom void of any activity today?

Modern research suggests poltergeist activity is actually generated by a secondary personality who unknowingly uses paranormal abilities to produce the phenomena. Usually this involves a female just entering puberty.

Some paranormal researchers expand on this theory and suggest that a person undergoing physical or mental trauma may unconsciously produce a force called psychokinetic energy. This power, if released, might cause paranormal happenings such as poltergeist activity.

What most researchers agree is that poltergeists are not in fact ghosts and tend to be more malicious and destructive than ghosts. They are nonhuman entities, not the returned spirits of the deceased. Ghosts and poltergeists are often confused or misidentified because they both produce phenomena such as unidentifiable rapping, footsteps, voices, and levitating objects.

If the happenings of the 1970's were down to this phenomenon where and when did the story of the murderous monk begin? If Diane Pritchard had in fact been the innocent culprit behind the activity why then should the house continue to offer activity no one has, as yet, been fully able to explain? Why was the moment lost when on two separate occasions, activity was at its height? The Enfield haunting several years later produced nationwide interest and was documented thoroughly. Why had this not been the case with East Drive?

Looking back I feel the true story had been sadly missed. Hearsay combined with folklore seems to have set the seal and the legend was cemented for generations to come.

The rest of the night for us held no terror. No dark robed figures graced our presence and we gradually felt at ease with the house. Mobile telephones were used for audio recording and we spent the small hours engaged in idle conversation. Whenever we were sat downstairs intermittent bangs and mysterious footsteps continued to resound above and when we were in the bedrooms the same noises were clearly heard below. 'Fred' it seemed was shy and preferred a game of cat and mouse with us rather than the full frontal assault he chose almost forty years ago, but I suppose we were 3 men strong and not a lone teenage girl.

Another dawn chorus of blackbirds and song thrushes heralded the end to our second night's vigil as dawn slowly crept over the night sky. Despite no dramatic events during the night, we felt satisfied we had collected sufficient evidence to further our investigation. Careful to leave the house in a tidy state we collected the seven empty cans of lemonade consumed earlier and put them on the kitchen work surface. As we sat in the living room debriefing, a metallic sound was clearly heard from the kitchen. Collectively we sprang up and rushed to get into the empty kitchen. The empty cans were still on the work surface but were now laid out in a single, straight line, the middle one crushed inwards from its centre.

Having personally randomly put the empty drinks cans on the work surface, I knew I hadn't left them as they were now.

Firework displays always end with a finale and for us the house had now offered up its own crescendo. It would have been impossible for anyone to have secretly entered the house, arranged the empty drinks containers and left between the sound being heard by us and our arrival in the kitchen seconds later. Again we were confused. A delicate and precise arrangement of aluminium objects was not usually the work of demonic entities making their presence known to scare the living. Poltergeists, unless my own research was wrong, were never precise and more often verged on chaotic destruction. If this was the work of 'Fred' then it was obvious he was both playful and mischievous and this latest unexplained phenomenon proved this.

Now weary with growing fatigue we once again closed and locked up the front door but left with more questions than answers.

The following week I looked through countless photographs and listened to the recorded audio footage we had captured. Several of the photographs especially from the bedroom once used by Philip Pritchard, the staircase and living room showed round circular light abnormalities often referred to as spiritual orbs. These balls of light are often thought to be the souls of people. Most orb images however, are caused by the camera flash, or light of some sort reflecting from something such as glass, mirrors, metal, walls, dust, pollen, and even moisture. Validity of the photographs had to be substantiated. We needed proof and any explanation which could be scientifically explained was simply no good for the book. Despite looking awesome the orbs captured were sadly discarded to the recycle bin, never to enjoy public viewing.

The audio recordings however were different. We were in the main bedroom and nothing seemed to be happening to support the house's haunted reputation. Impatient for evidence I suggested we should wait another five minutes and then go downstairs into the living room. Playback on the recording clearly makes out an unidentified female voice say 'yes I think so too, what do you think?' Even stranger, a man's voice is recorded saying 'yes downstairs is best'.

I simply could not explain the voices interrupting our conversation. The recording was taken through the simple capabilities of a mobile telephone and at that point we were not privy to any radio station scanning devices said to encourage voices and communication with those on a different spiritual level. The voices were real on the recording but had never been part of the original conversation.

The recordings gave evidence to suggest whatever was present within the house seemed to gain energy from human interaction. Whenever we sat in silence for periods of time simply listening in darkness the audio playback offered nothing in the way of spirit activity. Break times however, when we relaxed and chatted about everyday subjects were different. Short snippets of background conversations could be momentarily heard. It almost seemed as if it was us that were being investigated and scrutinised by an unseen audience.

For me this was proof East Drive was haunted. By a child killer Black Monk, or poltergeists or what, was a question I needed answering. The voices on the recording would seem to indicate other spirits were either visiting the property or were in occupation. From simple beginnings of investigating and writing about one alleged spirit we were now faced with the fact there was something else going on and possibly other entities were also haunting the property.

The house became a magnet pulling us in and was too great to dismiss and as each day passed I felt the need to re-visit gain strength. Within a week arrangements had been put in place for another overnight stay.

The date was once again set but this time we needed independent witnesses. Friends have a habit of colluding and collusion for the book would be open to both criticism and suggested fakery of any evidence collected.

For anyone remotely computer literate Facebook has become an alternative to telephone conversations, emails and more alarmingly face to face chat with those we know. I was familiar with this social network site and a friend on there, suggested I join 'Spooky Goings on in Yorkshire.' This is a great web page for anyone interested in the paranormal. No one posting, claims to be an expert. They are merely believers in what they have experienced personally. Although Yorkshire based it is a site open to everyone.

Interest in East Drive was evidently growing and my post was soon answered with numerous requests asking to join us on our next visit. Most had seen the movie and wanted more information about the research we were currently undertaking. Out of interest I made contact with one regular on the page who expressed an interest to visit the property. The following day Julie replied and thanked me for the invite. Both her and husband, Lee, were into all things paranormal and wished to join us on our next vigil. We agreed on a Friday night and arranged to meet on the street adjacent to the house.

Despite our earlier overnight vigils my heart was racing as I parked the car just off the roundabout. The semi-detached house appeared unchanged from when the reputed Black Monk had wreaked havoc and carnage forty years ago. One of the vertical blinds upstairs in the small bedroom was clearly pulled away almost as though unseen eyes were viewing the scene below. This phenomenon was not new; we had been told police call outs were numerous as vigilant neighbours' reported seeing movement in the windows of the empty house.

Julie and Lee arrived and it was obvious they were thinking along the same lines as ourselves. They believed in the paranormal but would only totally believe if there was no other rational explanation. As independent witnesses they would prove invaluable as the night progressed.

Inspection of each and every room evidenced nothing had changed since our last visit. We did however discover the house retained an electricity supply and the kettle was capable of boiling water. With haste I drove to the nearby row of shops and purchased coffee, milk and sugar.

Sitting in the lounge, drinking hot coffee, stirred with a pen, as no spoon could be found anywhere in the kitchen, we discussed the Black Monk.

The local legend said the monk had a liking for young girls. This liking had evolved into sexual deviance and eventually a local girl had disappeared. Found later raped and then murdered, to silence any evidence to convict the evil perpetrator.

Thankfully Steve was recording everything with his growing arsenal of mobile phones. On play back, Lee was clearly heard speaking about the monk and the fact that if you believe him to be evil then he will be evil.

As Lee spoke we could hear a women's voice say 'get me out now…………..the bender'

Immediately we played the recording back. The voice was not the voice of any one present. It was female, well spoken, calm and with an air of authority. There was no question this seemed to be a warning to others. Within seconds an acrid aroma could be smelt. On investigation this foul smell seemed to be coming from the floor immediately in front of the fireplace in the living room where we were sat. Within minutes the room became unbearable and we retreated to the kitchen. Imagine a public urinal not cleaned for years. This is what the living room at East Drive smelt like. I had worked as a coal miner for seventeen years and knew well the smell of stale urine. We had no toilets underground so communal areas were often used for toiletry needs. Never, however, had I experienced such a smell which made my eyes water. But within fifteen minutes the smell was gone. No trace anywhere in the house gave any hint of where the putrid odour came from. Outside areas around the house offered no explanation so drain problems were ruled out.

Was this the same odour the Pritchard family had described as being 'farmyard smells?' Given everyone present had recoiled almost in unison this could not simply have been the imagination of one person. How could something so pungent simply appear and just as quickly disappear? No atmospheric change in the house had been triggered with the opening of any windows or doors until the smell had receded and we checked outside for answers.

Several hours later we experienced similar phenomena. After having spent time upstairs we decided to take a break and make some more coffee. Once again the living room was engulfed in an unbearable smell. This time however the smell was different. Dog lovers know, only too well, the unmistakable pungent scent of wet fur regardless of how clean they keep their pet. The smell of 'wet dog' is like nothing else and it was this smell which permeated into every corner of the room. As before this was again overpowering and everyone was forced to take shelter in the comfort of the kitchen until the 'wet dog' smell subsided as quick as it had materialised and the room returned to normal.

Activity over the following couple of hours centred almost entirely on Julie and Lee filming orbs in two of the three bedrooms. Whether or not these are the work of paranormal activity or simply dust particles highlighted in the glare of digital photography remains a question to be verified.

The aerial flying display was impressive and over the next few weeks I replayed the video footage over and over again. Tiny balls of light appear to shoot from every direction, some following straight lines and others twisting, curving and changing direction. I have never claimed to be a paranormal investigator and continue to retain my innocence within this field. For me these orbs are inexplicable and have been added to an ever growing list of things in my life I do not understand.

Sometime after midnight, Julie and Lee took respite from the vigil and over a flask of stewed tea, played back the photographs taken on their digital camera. A series of shots taken in the parents' bedroom created intense excitement. One photograph distinctively portrayed the reflection of an unknown figure in the dressing table mirror. Despite only being of shadow form it appeared to be wearing some sort of baggy tunic and holding a straight pole which seemed to be cradled in a solid pouch at its crutch. Shots immediately before and after, showed no shadow or abnormality and our attempts to replicate the photograph, failed. Later inspection at home on the computer suggested the figure could have been that of a flag bearer from the famous battle on the grounds the house now stood upon. If this is correct, it remains a mystery as to why the figure appeared now on the first floor, four metres above what today, is ground level.

At approximately 2am my own personal beliefs about 30 East Drive changed.

Everybody was upstairs and the only lighting was that of an orange bulb above the staircase. Several bulbs of the same colour were stored in kitchen drawers and online images suggested these had been used in photo shoots to promote the film.

Julie and Lee were in the bathroom; Steve was in the bedroom once belonging to Philip Pritchard, and I was next door in what would have been the parents' bedroom.

'Bloody hell,' Steve's heavy Barnsley accent broke the silence, 'I've got a chuffin werewolf.'

First into the room I found Steve sat on the bed as I had left him just ten minutes before. In excited haste he reached out, the camera held firmly in his grasp. He quickly played back the last images he had taken and it was the final one which made the hairs on my neck and arms immediately rise with inner fear.

Although slightly blurred the photograph depicted a human-like form, stood within the doorway, facing the bathroom. The black shape however was not truly humanoid and could not be attributed to anyone present in the house.

Despite human in form it was obvious whatever had been digitally captured was not like anything I had seen before.

Stood upright it seemed to be floating slightly above the floor as if having both feet amputated at the ankles. The torso appeared to be extremely slim and sinewy and was leaning slightly forwards and its arms were bent at a ninety degree angle at the elbows as if some kind of karate stance. The slightly elongated head was also bent forwards, looking down as if in prayer.

None of us had any explanation as to what the figure could be. Every rational explanation was explored. Each in turn posed at the exact same spot and photographed using the same camera. Nothing of any likeness could be recreated and we estimated the figure stood at approximately seven feet tall when compared to our own sizes in proportion to the original photograph.

A coffee break was agreed and we sat downstairs trying in vain to explain the photograph. But before long the morning chorus of bird song filtered through the double glazed windows and doors and a unanimous decision was made to go home.

Before we said goodbye to 30 East Drive, on the path, in front of the house, we took the time to reflect on our experiences. Julie and Lee, obviously, had enjoyed the experience as much as I had. They had a joint interest in the paranormal and were not disappointed with the overnight stay. For me, their company was invaluable. As strangers, they were independent witnesses and avoided any speculation of collaboration between friends.

The following week I spent as much time as I could listening to the audio recordings and viewing the visual recordings. The woman's voice 'get me out now…………..the bender' I admit was a strange one to explain. Bender for me represented local slang for a drinking spree or a homosexual.

Colin Wilson, in his own investigation made reference to a Doctor Hans Bender, a well-known German parapsychologist from the Freiberg Institute. Hans had offered advice and his experience which was included in the original book. Was this 'the Bender' now referred to within the house?

Was this recorded voice a connection to our own investigation and the research carried out by Colin for his book 'Poltergeist?'

Other recordings were just as clear and all seemed to manifest when there was a conversation taking place. Nothing audible was played back from any of the mobile phones left unattended in a vacant room.

Probably one of the clearest voices was what I refer to as the 'pirate.' We were all seated in the kitchen drinking coffee. Julie is clearly heard speaking and out of nowhere a distinct voice can be heard saying 'Come here.' The dialect is what I would class as being southern, gruff and for me was the stereotypical retort of a 1950's Hollywood pirate.

Religion had never been discussed between myself and Steve and it was a surprise when he informed me he had contacted a Catholic priest in America. This priest was not your ordinary preacher however. Several years ago a movie had been released about exorcism rites performed by the Vatican. The script was based on true accounts of a young American priest sent to Italy to learn the ancient ritual of expelling demons from living human victims. The priest was impressed with the figure we had captured on the upstairs landing. His response was that if we owned the property then it demanded that a full exorcism should be carried out by the Catholic Church.

For me this response changed everything. From naivety and innocence the quest changed course dramatically. What simply began as a local story exploded into something not easy to comprehend. The original hauntings were dismissed by the local church as being the work of over stretched imagination and

69

trickery. Forty years later with one photograph the response was very different.

Excited by this I sent the same photograph to a respected and well know paranormal author who specialises in demonology. The following morning I received this answer.

'Hi Andy, It's unusual to me in that I have never before seen an anomalous photo that shows a defined bottom end. Usually the forms, whatever they are, dissipate at the bottom incomplete. I don't know any details about the case itself, though I am familiar with a lot of Colin Wilson's work. Good you have saved the SD card.'

For me this was the icing on the cake. Myth, folklore, and local history formed instantly to cement the story finally.

Unfortunately the photograph taken by Steve could not be included in the book due to copyright. Steve is an artist and intends to use the image as a back drop to his latest work.

30 East Drive was haunted. I am not psychic, a ghost hunter or in cahoots with other realms unknown to mankind. I am however a natural investigator. Having spent twenty years researching the history of my grandfather, despite all records having been destroyed and his own change of identity I had finally uncovered his story.

For me now The Black Monk was real. Who he was and what he was now, was the focus of my investigation. This was no longer a wild goose chase or a flight of fantasy. Something at East Drive generated energy unknown to the living. Poltergeist, Demon or ghost? This was the question which was now the focus of my attention and new found beliefs.

Chapter Four
Unanswered Questions

Thankfully no ghosts followed me home. 'Fred', it seemed, was happy to stay within the walls of 30 East Drive.

Chequerfield is an area rich in history. Siege works had been excavated years before on the outskirts of the area overlooking the nearby castle. The sprawling estate of council houses gave away little of the ground's bloody past and I doubt all but a fraction of the local population knew of the historical importance which lay beneath the neat tree lined avenues and closes. In 1644 on the 1st of March Sir Marmaduke Langdale led a Royalist army to success at the Battle of Chequerfield, Pontefract. The success of this battle lifted the First Siege of Pontefract Castle.

The whole area was open to paranormal activity and for me many questions needed answering.

The original hauntings of the 1960's and 1970's had pointed the finger of blame to a black habited monk. The story of The Black Monk of Pontefract reigned supreme and was unchallenged from the very beginning. The Pritchard family were the very first to witness this ghostly apparition and initially named him 'Mister Nobody' and later as simply 'Fred'.

Local historian and paranormal investigator Tom Cuniff had visited the Pritchard home sometime in the mid 1970's and researched the story. He suggested the

73

apparition could be a remnant from the local priory which had existed from 1090-1539, and whose gallows were just across the hill from the Pritchard home.

Mr Cuniff proposed in his writings that a monk had existed during Henry the Eighth's reign and was hanged for the rape and murder of a young girl. He concluded the poltergeist activity focused on Diane Pritchard who at the time was reaching puberty and could be interpreted as sexual in nature. In his writings he recorded having read archived documents to support this ancient crime. Unfortunately Colin Wilson in his own book 'Poltergeist' seemed to accept this piece of evidence as fact, thus cementing and reinforcing the story.

I needed evidence for validity and could not rely on speculation, hear-say or false information. If in fact a monk had committed an act of paedophilia in such an important stronghold as Pontefract then this would have been recorded.

Despite endless efforts I can find only one record of any individual connected to the church being hanged in the town.

George Beaumont vicar at the nearby South Kirkby Church was executed for 'treason' by the Roundheads after assisting local Royalists to recapture Pontefract Castle from the Parliamentarian forces. He was hanged before the walls of the castle in 1649 leaving a widow and four small children 'with but little sustenance'.

The next question for me was the reference to Father Michael. In the western church, a non-ordained monk is called a brother, a monk can be a priest, in which case he is called father, but not all monks are priests. This adds credence to my theory that the reference 'monk' was ill advised from the very beginning.

When the activity returned in 1974 it was said the daughter was now the focus of the poltergeist activity and it seemed it was her encroaching puberty which once again stirred whatever entity had taken residence within the house. In the book 'Poltergeist' Colin Wilson recorded accounts from the family which depicted a black robed monk as being the source of the haunting. Had the monk who was aroused sexually by the innocent virginal underage girls somehow carried this evil lust beyond the grave? The earthly life taken in execution but a need for sexual gratification and satisfaction relived without the fear of reprisal. Most criminals fear the thought of capture. If however the criminal could continue unheeded after death why then does the fear of death fill them with the same dread as it does the righteous? Commit a crime in life and face punishment, commit the same crime in death and remain free of any form of retribution and punishment.

I was now far from content with the evidence and information collected on the history. The property was certainly haunted but finally the truth needed to be sort. The Black Monk story raised pockets of doubt as I began to filter the pros and cons of what we had collected so far. Records survive of a Cluniac order of monks present in the area dating back to 1090AD. I did not have access to first-hand accounts from the family and so I had to respect their reported personal beliefs of what originally occurred.

If the unexplained activity was indeed the work of a sex crazed Cluniac Monk why would he suddenly appear to terrorise a family on two separate occasions spanning almost a decade? If the spiritual energy was at such a level that a young girl could be dragged upstairs by the throat then why did it dissipate to such a level the family could continue to live within the house for another thirty years? The books I have read on alleged true hauntings tended to evidence the spiritual culprits being there for the long haul. East Drive was different. Two short spells of violent activity and then nothing. Three questions for me needed answering. Why did the hauntings suddenly occur? Why was a normal, everyday working class family the target? Why did the activity suddenly cease?

The evidence and eye witness accounts were too numerous to discredit as being false. East Drive was not your ordinary semi-detached house, despite its normal setting on the leafy street outside.

This story could never be captured within the pages of a few chapters of any book. Earlier references to this particular haunting accepted the basics without sifting fact from fiction. Despite being armed with little technology boasted by other supposed 'ghost hunters' I had one piece of armour up my sleeve. Rational thinking was my firepower combined with dogged determination. Whatever phenomena I could replicate within the house was to be dismissed and no reference would be made available for my book.

Chapter Five
Stepping into the Abyss

The stage was now set and East Drive was becoming an addiction I found harder and harder to resist. After each visit an inner craving to return grew stronger and it felt strangely comforting whenever the door opened. I was not alone, both Steve and Glynn also admitted to feeling this draw to the property. Despite the infamy surrounding East Drive the house somehow felt welcoming and comfortable. Most of the furniture, despite not being original to the Pritchard family fitted well into the atmosphere. Purchased from local charity shops the theme of 1970's Yorkshire was continued forty years on and any visitor could easily be fooled they had stepped back in time. It was easy to simply close your eyes and mentally listen to the opening chorus of Thursday nights Top of the Pops whilst taking in the spicy aromas of a 'Vesta', ready to cook, Indian meal simmering on the gas fuelled hob.

Our next visit soon came and once again I found myself in familiar surroundings. Nothing seemed out of place from our last visit but it was obvious other visitors had visited the property. Once again in each room there were pieces of lined paper and a penny. Around the pennies a circle had been drawn. Despite not being an expert in paranormal investigations I knew these were trigger objects often used by groups seeking evidence of ghostly happenings. Most of the coins remained within their circles however some had moved and were offset from their ink circumferences. Again this was evidence I could not accept as factual so had to be discarded. The coins could have been purposely moved to fool or simply have been affected by natural phenomena such as vibration from passing traffic and the weight of people walking close by. Mining subsidence also needed to be taken into account. Deep beneath Pontefract rich coal seams had been extracted leaving vast areas empty of geological voids where the coal had been taken. These empty spaces in time obey gravity and the land above drops and settles accordingly creating shifting movement in various stages and severity.

If indeed the Black Monk of Pontefract was a fearsome poltergeist to be feared and avoided at all cost then the ability to move coins was for me a disappointment. For the book I needed fear and dread. I never wished to be dragged up the stairs by the throat as in the original haunting but I did expect more from whatever occupied the house.

Again the inner child within me reigned supreme and I had lost the battle. Writing the book now took second place and for me importance lay within uncovering the mystery. I now purchased two motion detector alarms and it was agreed we would set them in the two main bedrooms overlooking the staircase. I was dubious about the sensitivity of the detectors. Experimenting at home I concluded any movement would have to be significant to trigger the audible alarm.

We decided to set one of the alarms in what had been Philip Pritchard's bedroom and close the door to eliminate any movement from outside the room. The second alarm was positioned downstairs in the living room pointing towards the glass panelled door at the bottom of the stairs. With both rooms locked off we settled ourselves into the kitchen to discuss a plan for the night ahead. Within ten minutes the loud, high pitched alarm resounded from the motion detector upstairs. Collectively we hurried upstairs to disarm the apparatus. No sooner was silence resumed the detector downstairs gave out its signal that movement had been detected in the closed down stairs living room.

This same game of cat and mouse continued well into the night. One detector sounded, was deactivated only for the other to warn us of movement within its own 180 degree movement sensor.

Whatever was triggering movement wanted to divide us. We decided however to stay together and use joint wisdom against whatever unseen forces were surrounding us. We now set both motion detectors upstairs. The one night vision camcorder we had at our disposal was placed immediately behind one of the detectors.

On cue the audio alarm broke the silence. Video footage was instantly played back and it recorded the motion detector turning slowly to the right. It now faced the wall. Excitement exploded within me. I now had raw footage of the poltergeist. The motion detector clearly turns almost ninety degrees and on playback it is evident no-one enters the room.

Like everything we capture either visual or audible we try to replicate it for authenticity. Only what cannot be reproduced would we record as being unexplained activity which could be attributed evidence of a true haunting. Glynn raised his concern the glass topped bedside cabinet on which the sensor sat could have acted as a low friction slide exaggerated by the high pitched alarm. We tested this theory immediately and sure enough the motion detector, once activated slowly began to turn clockwise towards the wall. Disappointment now replaced excitement. Vibration from the audible alarm caused the rotation. One small glimmer of hope however prevailed. On playback movement was detected seconds before the alarm sounded. It was impossible an inanimate object could predict something which would have an effect on it. Unfortunately despite this the evidence had to be put onto the back burner.

With heavy hearts we once again focused our attentions on the night ahead. Mobile telephones were placed both upstairs and in the kitchen and left to record without contamination of human interference.

Conversation focused on the original story of the Black Monk. We now knew from eyewitness accounts there was a capped off well which lay beneath the foundations of the house and its perimeter extended next door. Phil Bates a local man recounted first hand sight of this when council workmen were repairing damage to the semi-detached property's living room floor. A childish desire to explore had taken him beneath the wooden floorboards and he recalled seeing the ancient capping stone covering the wells interior.

Despite this the hanging of the sex crazed monk remained puzzling. If this was in fact true, why would the perpetrators discard his dying body into a well? If mob rule had taken place and justice carried out according to such a vile act against a child then why would they destroy a source of much needed drinking water. A rotting corpse would make the well useless. Surely in the days long before forensic science there would have been countless ways to dispose of a body. The story simply did not hold water. Doubts leaked at every angle and something was not right with the story that had been told for over forty years.

Deep in contemplation the serenity of the moment was shattered with another high pitched retort from one of the motion detectors upstairs. Realising the lateness of the hour and knowing Carol next door had grandchildren asleep, panic washed over me. Children need sleep and regardless of what danger the house presented I immediately rose from the settee and began making my way speedily upstairs to silence the deafening high pitched intruding decibels. Halfway up the carpeted staircase I was stopped in my tracks.

Momentarily I was transported to my days underground as a coal miner. In one split second I saw the unsupported roof collapsing above me. Darkness descended as if a totally black mass was spewing over the heavily painted white wooden landing rail. My inner 'pit sense' took over and my body went into auto pilot. I crouched into the foetal position and waited for the inevitable. The killing blow of falling rock, however, never came. I was not to be recorded as yet another fatality lost to win the price of coal. As quickly as the utter blackness appeared it retreated and normality returned. Panic and fear within me subsided and I regained composure. Despite the darkness the ceiling above me could be seen and now joined by Glynn we were able to ascend the stairs and silence the motion detector.

Complete and utter darkness was something I was trained for. Each year it was mandatory training for everyone to practice putting on the 'self-rescuer' every miner carried on his belt. This piece of apparatus offered ninety minutes survival in the event of a fire and lethal carbon monoxide poisoning. To make the training authentic the drill had to be carried out under total darkness without any contamination of artificial light. What I experienced on the staircase of East Drive surpassed anything I experienced underground. This was not merely dark but something blacker than anything I can describe. The density was so intense it seemed impenetrable as if made of solid matter the like of which I had never before seen.

I was momentarily shaken with an inner feeling of fear and dread never before experienced. This was beyond anything normal and I would never again wish to experience anything like it again. For just a few seconds it seemed I was lost in a wave of blackness and unexplainable despair.

Thankfully the invention of 240 volt household electricity and a simple forty amp bulb helped rebuild bravado as we took brief respite in the kitchen. Strong coffee helped to restore confidence and we once again were ready to resume the vigil.

We decided upstairs would now be the best place to position ourselves. The black mass could still be present so it was logical if any evidence was to be caught then the first floor was the place to be. We decided to disarm the motion detectors. Despite not being too sensitive as I found in my experiments at home they were readily picking movement up in most rooms we placed them. The cat and mouse game of arm and silence could continue throughout the night and ruin any chance of collecting further evidence of unexplained activity within the house.

The equipment we had in our arsenal was still primitive but enthusiasm overcame and we settled ourselves in the master bedroom.

Despite the house having an electricity supply we agreed no artificial lighting should be used wherever possible. Cautiously we settled ourselves on the double bed, still bare of sheets or pillows the ageing mattress did offer some comfort. The 1970's / 1980's wall to wall wardrobe, moulded and mirrored, was probably authentic and original to the Pritchard family. The relic of bygone fashion of four doors, mirrors and plastic ornate surround was simply something not fashionable today. The cheap and outdated teak dressing table was an obvious addition to the house, probably purchased at very little cost from one of the nearby charity shops. Thankfully the individual vertical blinds covering the window allowed some light into the room from the nearby street lamps and we could at least see each other's faces.

At first we sat in silence simply taking in the atmosphere of the house. Momentarily I felt a strange feeling of sadness wash over me. The house held such a violent reputation of paranormal activity but for me it felt lonely and deserted, a relic of some bygone forgotten age. It was like meeting a world heavyweight champion fighter many years after his final victorious bout in the ring. The name was not forgotten but the aging body offered only weakness and merely a shadow of its former self, its former glory.

Occasional knocks and bangs could be heard from downstairs but without the motion detectors these could not be attributed to anything other than natural sounds of the house.

Nothing in the room indicated ghostly activity and after a brief discussion it was agreed we should again take a break and go downstairs.

With cups replenished with hot coffee we sat and discussed again the story of the monk. Thankfully the mobile phone had recorded our conversation upstairs. Our voices can clearly be heard discussing the absence of ghostly activity. The audio playback, however, gave us something we did not expect. My own voice is clearly heard saying that we should have another five minutes in the bedroom then perhaps take the vigil downstairs where most of the banging noises seemed to be coming from. Even clearer than my own voice someone replies,

'Yes I think so, what do you think?' Stunned and before we could comment another unknown voice replies,

'I agree downstairs seems best.' Disbelief filled each and every one of us. The two voices were not only invisible intruders but they were openly joining our conversation, even giving their opinions as to what, they thought, was the best option for us to next. We repeatedly played back the recording and picked up another voice this time that sounded like a well-spoken woman. Unlike the other two voices this did not engage in our conversation and is heard saying,

'Get down..........Evil.'

Like excited children playing with a new toy for the first time we played back the recording over and over again until the battery in the mobile phone gave up, exhausted from over use.

We could not offer any single piece of rational explanation for the phenomena recorded. None of the three voices sounded anything like the voice of anybody present. There was no television or radio being played. Nothing in the house was capable of creating anything remotely resembling what we recorded. With this we decided to call it a day and end the vigil. We had captured more than we bargained for and for us this was more than enough.

Just before daybreak we decided to spend some final time in darkness in the living room. I positioned myself in the armchair next to the French doors, Steve taking rest on the settee opposite. Before long Steve's voice broke the silence,

'Andy, tha's not gunna believe this, what's just gone past here. Never seen owt like it...... It weren't an orb.'

'Have you got in on camera?' I asked.

'Yes, am sure I have, I must have.'

The video footage was strange to say the least. I am clearly seen in the armchair and two disc like objects, hand size, float across the room, joining together as they pass me at knee height. We repeatedly played back the twenty seven second clip and could offer no rational explanation. The discs it seems maintain a set height and speed as they cross the room in an exact straight line. No deviation can be seen as is usually the case with orb footage. Only when the battery finally drained of energy did we focus our attentions on calling a final end to the night.

We did a final walk-through of each room to make sure nothing had been left behind and bade our farewell to 'Fred' before locking the door. Despite the lateness and dark of the night, the semi-detached house was bathed in an artificial glow offered from nearby street lighting. The exterior of the house seemed even more foreboding than its interior as we slowly drove away.

Chequerfield at night seemed so different to the busy estate of daylight hours. Each and every darkened street felt as if there was some tightly guarded secret held tight within the very ground. Bricks and mortar now covering historical barbarity were simply a disguise to the real nature of this raised expanse of ground. 30

East Drive was in no way the centre of haunting activity. As we slowly made our way out of the estate it was obvious the very earth held up to the hauntings. Blood once ran freely into the absorbent soil and for centuries it was this lifeblood which fed the crops of old.

The whole of the Chequerfield Estate held for me the same uncertainty 30 East Drive presented. In darkness the area felt very different. Gone were the friendly tree lined avenues. Now darkness seemed to offer something more sinister. Momentarily each and every shadow seemed to move with an unseen activity to lost eyes no longer visible. It took little imagination to hear the volleys of cannon fire descending onto the mighty castle below and I fought desperately to keep my attention on the road ahead.

Thankfully the slow descent into the town of Pontefract released all thoughts of ill feeling and suffering. Taxi drivers hurried about their business of transporting drunken revellers to their homes after a night of drinking and dancing in the many public houses Pontefract was still renowned for. I found comfort in the company of headlights along the way and it was a final relief when I finally reached the comfort and safety of home.

Despite all that had happened at East Drive I found sleep easily as the duvet offered warmth and solace. No sooner had my eyelids closed when the irritating high pitched call of the battery operated alarm clock woke me. Time offers no mercy to the weary and it was with resentment I slowly forced myself from the warm bed and quickly dressed for another day at work.

Rigours of the modern working day offered no time for me to think about the happenings encountered during the previous night. Once home my time was limited so it took almost a week to fully work my way through the recordings we had captured during our overnight stay.

Our journey had begun with little thought as to what we might encounter and it was now I felt a little lost. My inner self and beliefs leant towards an inner acceptance of spirits. Ghosts were real and a natural process of birth, life and death. Without personal proof, however, the shadow of doubt had always veiled my own final belief of what was real and what was not.

True belief now outweighed disbelief and I knew from the material we already had in our possession paranormal activity was not something we could simply dismiss as over active imagination or trickery. What began as simply a desire to record alleged local hauntings to create a book for entertainment had changed. The pages were now to record a true account of a very real haunting never before explored or told in its true entirety.

30 East Drive had captured me and I knew there was something deep within the very fabric of the place which had evaded others before me, searching for the truth. I had come to the conclusion that only the surface had been scratched and it was time the full story was

uncovered and told (or as much as was humanly possible to do). I would try to finally piece the puzzle together.

Stories of the Black Monk remained doubtful and I was now on my own quest for the truth.

Chapter Six
Loading the Guns

I truly wanted to believe in the story of the Black Monk. The tale was ingrained into my childhood and had placed, for generations, where I live on the map. Ask visitors to the area about the Featherstone Massacre and chances are they will offer up just a blank expression. Ask the same people if they know anything about the Poltergeist of Pontefract and they can often relate to the story and the recent film. It is sad that true suffering and loss slips from memory whereas tales of ghostly happenings seem to stick in the minds of many.

During the next four months I wrote very little. East Drive had captured me and I was ever drawn to my next opportunity to stay at the house. Lack of time was not the only burden and I was now becoming financially involved in seeking out the truth. If I were to go further with the investigation I needed the correct tools to record and scrutinise anything I could not explain during the visits.

Amazon and EBay are both a fantastic open marketplace for the consumer. Unfortunately paranormal research still relies on a system of either belief or disbelief. No common denominator exists between the never ending suppliers of equipment and some people who prey on the unwary.

After each visit I found myself researching the best equipment available suiting my small pockets. As proof of the paranormal was yet to be validated the apparatus was simply on a test basis, regardless of the supplier's claims.

Eventually I decided to purchase a spirit box. A Spirit Box is an audio-only device which quickly scans through multiple radio channels and is claimed to make it relatively easy for spirits to manipulate the frequencies to say a word or phrase in real time

Paranormal researchers claim white noise helps spirits form words and phrases which can either be heard at the time or through recorded playback. I needed more evidence, so for me this was an item I needed in my ghost hunting arsenal of equipment. Trying not to waste money, I had researched all the tools for attempting communication with paranormal entities and decided to purchase a P-SB7 custom made device, which according to countless online reviews, was the most accurate and reliable Spirit Box currently on the market. Below is the product description which finally clinched the deal for me.

'The B-PSB7 Spirit Box creates compact frequency sweeps to generate white noise which theories suggest give some entities the energy they need to be heard. When this occurs you will sometimes hear voices or sounds coming through the static in an attempt to communicate.

While this unit does have FM and AM sweep modes, the power has been specifically focused on the FM side for greater FM amplification. Because of this, some refer to this model as AM detuned. This provides more white noise energy through FM. By focusing this power in that direction, the AM side is now clear from white noise providing greater clarity while sweeping. This unit utilizes a milli-second adjustable forward or reverse frequency 'sweep' technique coupled with a proprietary high frequency synthetic noise or 'white noise' distributed between frequency steps.'

For me this was a must purchase. I needed recorded proof of paranormal activity within the house as well as photographic and video material.

Unfortunately the Spirit Box needed additional apparatus to work effectively. The inbuilt speaker offered little volume so my next purchase was an additional speaker. If I were now to prove contact with spirit I also needed to record this for later playback and evidence. At further cost I invested in a digital Dictaphone with inbuilt memory and USB capability enabling the device to be plugged into a computer for file transfer.

Still not entirely happy I had everything I needed for the job in hand my next purchase was a strobe light.

A strobe light is a tool used in ghost investigating which simulates the shutter of a camera. The strobe light allows us to see things that usually would be moving too fast for the mind/eye to detect. Most 'ghost hunters' believe manifesting apparitions function on a higher vibration than those on the physical plane. The faster the strobe light, the more effectively it works in ghost investigations. Researchers are leaning toward the opinion that the strobe exercises the eyes and makes them more capable of seeing an apparition. This is particularly true when seeing 'shadow people' only seen with peripheral vision, seen out of the corner of the eye.

Like everything I buy, I first test it in the safe environment of home. The strobe light bothered me after about twenty minutes as I sat alone in the dark. My eyes felt strained and I found it difficult to remain focused for periods of more than ten minutes. I did however achieve success with my home experiment. I set up a night shot camcorder and deliberately threw armchair cushions across the room in front of the lens. Playback recorded something moving quickly across the artificial lighting of the equipment. With the strobe light I could clearly see the square dark shape of the cushion as it seemingly passes the camera in slow motion. Thankfully I do not suffer from epilepsy so for me the strobe could be used, albeit in short intervals.

The shopping spree continued and I found myself drawn to laser lighting. The marketing spiel captured me with the following claims.

'This high powered laser emits a grid of green dots useful for detecting shadows or general visual disturbances during an investigation. Set it in front of a running camera to catch potential evidence. You can adjust the size and shape of the stars by turning the adjustable lens. Detach the lens and it will function as a high powered laser pointer.'

Drawn immediately to the advertisement another sale was agreed and I waited like an impatient child for the arrival of yet another toy. The laser arrived within seven days and I was happy with my latest purchase.

With four attachable heads the laser grid offered different shapes and size of bright lights which, when used in a darkened room fill the entire facing wall with an array of bright green dots.

My granddaughter Ava found the laser pen highly amusing as she danced endlessly in front of the myriad of projected pinpricks of lights on the wall behind her. Her dance moves proved the gadget did exactly what the manufacturer claimed. Her every movement showed as a shadow on the wall and I was impressed in what proof could be captured in conjunction with video recording.

For me now the stage was set. If 'Fred' wanted to make an appearance I was ready. He had entered the paranormal stage long ago in the 1960's and 1970's when technology was at an infant stage. If now the infamous Black Monk was to drag me up the stairs by the throat then at least this would be on camera and recorded for the worldwide audience on YouTube to witness. Secretly, however, I did wish if anyone was to be dragged upstairs then Glynn should be the victim. Coward or not, but my survival overshadowed evidence. Besides, I thought, when it came to recording any evidence I was the quicker of the two to respond. In the interest of the book it would be practical if Glynn should then be the victim if anything occurred beyond our control.

I was still studying the countless photographs and audio recordings, before our next visit, although the majority of the photographic material proved inconclusive and was discarded.

Most photographs showed shapes and shadows which all of us can perceive as forming recognised objects. The audio recordings however were very different indeed.

Recordings preceded the ghost box purchase and were the product of simple mobile phone recordings. The voices were many and seemed to manifest mostly when we were engaged in conversation. The dialect seemed real but in the most was detracted from our own conversation. The well-spoken woman repeatedly came through warning of evil and for us to get out. Female children as if excited in play came through clambering for attention. For me the 'Miner' it was like being awarded the golden chalice. I could hardly believe the words my ears were picking up as I listened closely to the played back recording.

'Don't shine th' light on me.....' Could be clearly heard in a thick Yorkshire accent followed by, 'You keep thee gob shut!' The first sentence immediately struck a chord with me. The first seventeen years of my working life had been spent working deep underground as a coal miner. With artificial lighting installed only along the main thoroughfares of the main tunnels each miner was supplied with a powerful lamp which fastened to the front of his mandatory white safety helmet. The lights were quite powerful and it was an unwritten rule that you should avoid pointing the beam directly into the eyes of a fellow miner. Occasionally I had witnessed rising tensions between miners, usually over a disagreement on the rugby field or an accused 'slight-of-hand' at the card table the night before. As the pot of tension boiled over it was common for one of the men to break the rule and shine his lamp directly into the eyes of the other.

'Don't shine thee light on me!' was the trigger point indicating things were about to get ugly and if left, a fist fight was inevitable. Thankfully others would always intervene before the first punch was thrown and at the shift end both aggrieved parties would be seen in the pithead baths soaping down each other's backs.

For me this was proof a spirit of a former coal miner had made its presence known on that particular visit. I felt I was somehow now in good hands. In life, miners always looked after their own with an allegiance like that of a family. I doubted very much death would break this connection and perhaps I now had someone from the spirit world protecting my back. Together as miners we had risen against the full might of the Thatcher government in defiance against the unstoppable tyranny of ultimate power and control. Battered, bruised and forever scarred I survived the onslaught. 'Fred' I thought was now a less formidable character I could face without fear of unseen retribution. If a coal miner was in spirit then I had little to fear. Comradeship I believed would extend from beyond the grave.

Simple audio evidence indicated something was happening at East Drive which could not yet be explained. I still remained sceptical however of the original story. For me 30 East Drive was like being seated at a busy bus stop. You sit and listen to the conversations of others around you and catch just a glimpse into their lives. Without warning the next bus stops on route and familiar people leave. The void is replaced by others exiting the bus who takes turn to wait for the next bus.

I felt the house was a like a gateway, a bus stop if you will, into and out of a world we could not see.

Other ghost hunters do believe that portals exist between the physical and spirit worlds. It has been suggested that these portals could act as a doorway for ghosts and spirits to cross over from the other worlds into the physical realm. If they do exist, it is further speculated that hauntings and paranormal activity increase near these doorways into our world.

If this is true, could East Drive in fact be such a gateway? Would this explain why so many different voices were heard on the audio recordings?

If however there was a portal attached to the property why had this not been picked up from the days of the original activity?

Why also had no full investigation been undertaken to finally determine what was really happening. Why also at the height of poltergeist activity was the blame pointed at one entity in particular?

Perhaps it is just a measure of how we approach these events, these happenings today have opened our minds to more possibilities and have put our fears of what we don't understand to one side.

Secretly I began to think I had made a huge mistake. I always believed the Monk story to hold elements of truth and expected to write an updated version of his story. Innocently I had stumbled blindly into something that was far beyond my first ideas, something I did not understand and something I could not simply turn away from without delving deeper. I had cast the bait and the hook was taken. For me I now had no choice other than to reel in whatever it was I had recorded.

If 'Fred' had been the culprit the book would have been much easier to complete. With just one historical fact to research and verify this should have been a simple task. 'Fred' was no longer the total answer, if he was the answer at all, and I had begun to realise there was much more to the actual property that had never been questioned.

Continuing my research I came across an interesting article called 'The Philip Experiment'.

In the 1970's a group of Canadian parapsychologists wanted to attempt an experiment to create a ghost proving their theory the human mind can produce spirits through expectation, imagination and visualization.

The actual experiment took place in Toronto, Canada, in 1972, under the direction of the world-renowned expert on poltergeists, Dr A. R. G. Owen.

The members of the experiment proposed an idea. By using extreme and prolonged concentration, they could create their ghost through a collective thought form: Non-physical entities which exist in either the mental or astral plane. In order to create this ghost and make it as 'real' as possible, it needed a life story; a background which the ghost could 'relate' to.

They named the ghost they were attempting to bring into focus 'Philip Aylesford' and created a tragic story, explaining to the fullest and in great detail, his life, and the few actions that lead to his tragic death.

Step two was contacting Philip. In September 1972, the group began their 'sittings' and after some initial problems the group attempted to duplicate the atmosphere of a classic spiritualist séance. They dimmed the room's lights, sat around a table and surrounded themselves with pictures of the type of castle they imagined Philip would have lived in, as well as objects from that time period.

Within a few weeks, Philip made contact. Although he did not manifest in spiritual form, appearing as an apparition or ghost, he did make contact through a brief rap on the group's table. 'Philip' answered questions that were consistent with his fictitious history, but was unable to provide any information beyond that which the group had conceived. However, 'Philip' did give other historically accurate information about real events and people. The Owen group theorized that this latter information came from their own collective unconsciousness.

The sessions took off from there, producing a range of phenomena that could not be explained scientifically. His 'spirit' was able to move the table, sliding it from side to side. On more than one occasion, the table chased someone across the room. All hands were clear of the table when this occurred.

In conclusion the experimenters were never able to prove the 'how' and the 'why' behind Philip's manifestation. Was Philip a direct result of the group's collective subconscious or perhaps did they conjure an actual entity that simply latched onto the story?

While some would conclude that they prove that ghosts don't exist, that such things are in our minds only, others say that our unconscious could be responsible for this kind of the phenomena some of the time.

Another point of view is that even though Philip was completely fictional, the Owen group really did contact the spirit world. A playful (or perhaps demonic, some would argue) spirit took the opportunity of these séances to 'act' as Philip and produce the extraordinary psychokinetic phenomena recorded.

Whatever caused the manifestation it seems that it adapted itself to the expectation of the audience, playing the role of the spirit they intended to contact? Since all was based on fiction it could not be the spirit of Philip so what else could it be?

My question now was, was 'Fred' true to the story. Was he conjured up somehow in imagination and teenage excitement of the early 1970's? Like Philip he did have traces of truth behind his story. Pontefract is rich in history with records of monks working the land on what is now Chequerfield. There had been a Cluniac Priory located within one mile of the house and no doubt the castle held tightly guarded secrets, locked within its once impenetrable walls. If indeed a spirit was to make its mark then the guise of a black robed monk would be perfect. I make no suggestion that the experiment with 'Philip' had been replicated in any way but could the same thought process of innocent collectiveness create something similar? Did something far more sinister fill the void and take advantage of a doorway being opened by innocents not understanding what they were creating.

I would never doubt anything the family experienced whilst in residence. Their own horrors are thankfully long gone and personal to them. Their own story is best left to rest in the annals of time and the movie. Without doubt they had been terrorised on not just one but on two separate occasions spanning a period of six years. Interestingly both episodes occurred when the children were in puberty. Philip first followed by Diane later in 1974. Research into Poltergeist activity supports this connection, as does the activity remaining for just a short period of time. If this was indeed the case why then does activity, albeit on a much lower level, continue? If this was Poltergeist activity then surely the story could finally be put to rest. No teenagers reside now within the house and vacant of occupants there were no inner family feuds to feed any malevolent forces into crossing the gateway into the living world.
Despite this The Black Monk, however, cannot be ignored. Only one reference to 'Fred' can be found in existing historical records.

On Saturday, March 28, 1587 Frederick de Alcyonius aged forty seven and native of Pontefract was hanged, beheaded and quartered at St. Leonard's, Green Dykes at York. A crowd of eight thousand gathered to watch the spectacle which resulted in the decapitated head being set upon a spike on the fortified walls containing the town. The execution was set for 3.00pm. Records say this was a traitor's death. The crime for which Frederick was executed was 'petty treason'. Unfortunately, records of the North-Eastern Assize circuit for the Tudor period do not survive, so no further particulars of the crime were on record. Petty treason could however include the murder of a master by his servant. Were Frederick and 'Fred' connected? If this were true then whatever began haunting East Drive was either a figment of collective imagination or a deceiver.

Countless questions now blocked my path. Why had the original activity begun? The Pritchard family were only the second family to take up residence in the council property. The first tenants, for reasons unknown, had occupied the property for only a short period of time so in essence the Pritchard's were the first to make the house a family home. I have been informed by local residents 30 East Drive and the adjoining property were the last houses to be built on the new estate. Work on completion was hampered by thieves constantly stealing building material whenever the opportunity arose, if indeed it had been thieves? Had something been trying to stop the building being erected; just a thought!

If the building work had in fact disturbed an already existing gateway or portal why then would it take almost twenty years for an entity to manifest?

If poltergeist activity was the basis of whatever happened at the house why then would it manifest briefly in the late 1960's, cease, and then reoccur for several months in 1974?

Why would the happenings again resume in 2012 following the release of the film 'When the Lights Went Out?'

For me it seemed the common denominator was human belief in the paranormal. If 'Fred' was indeed conjured up with innocent adolescent minds could the same mind-set have opened a gateway to the spirit realm? Soil beneath East Drive was rich in blood and suffering and if human and spiritual barriers existed this would be the ideal location dividing the two. Life and death can be divided by seconds but separated forever. It was the connection between the two I now sought.

30 East Drive Chequerfield Pontfract. The house was built in the 1950's

Pontefract Castle would have been an imposing sight from the elevated position of Chequerfield

Despite all exterior doors being locked the bible had moved across the kitchen work surface.

Unexplained shadows which could not be replicated on subsequent visits to the house

Could this have been our first encounter with whatever entity lurked inside the house?

A small selection of the equipment used during researching the book.

Unexplained shadow only seen when the photograph were later scrutinised.

Historic map showing modern day East Drive to have once been the sight of a bloody battle

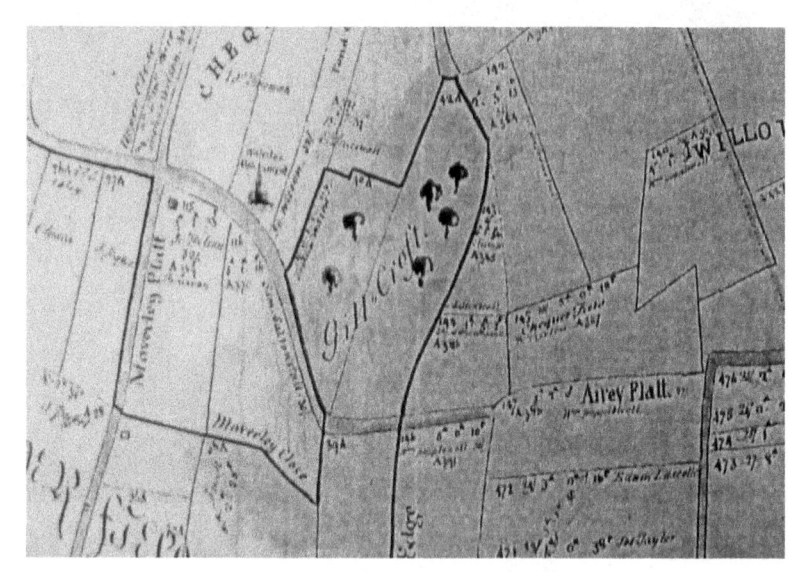

Hand drawn map from showing the area of East Drive to be enclosed with what appears to be an orchard

The site of what was then a pump is recorded on this map dating back to the early 1800's. Had the pump been a later addition to the existing well?

Chapter Seven
No Place Like Home

For the next ten months we spent at least one night a week at East Drive. Personally I now felt attached to the house and missed the days whenever I could not visit. When it came to the day of our next visit it strangely felt as if I had only momentarily left, I was returning home from a long day at work. The interior always gave a feeling of welcoming and it was difficult to comprehend reports of evil wrong doings ever playing a part in the house's history. It came as no surprise that Glynn revealed that he had the same feelings. He, too, was drawn to East Drive as if some magnetic force had been set to snare us. We were like schoolchildren drawn to something almost taboo. Although I was the younger, neither us would see the greener years of youth again. Both of us were level headed, to some degree, so I could not understand the boyish excitement we both experienced whenever we spoke about the house.

30 East Drive was becoming an addiction. We were now like innocent night club revellers who had been introduced to the euphoric effects of a drug for the very first time. Enjoying the experience so much we would return again the following week, but with each weekend gone the feeling of wanting more becomes ever present and temptation requires a midweek 'fix'. East Drive was now our addiction and we found ourselves spending extra time during daylight hours sitting within the four

walls trying to satisfy our quest for the final truth and closure.

Every visit gave us activity we could not explain whether it was in darkness or during daylight hours. The game of cat and mouse which began six months earlier on our first visit continued. Whenever we were in one room knockings or footsteps would be heard in another. Fluctuations in temperature occurred repeatedly. One moment the house felt comfortable and lived in and minutes later a feeling of dampness and abandonment filled the atmosphere.

Different odours also seemed to fill the living room despite all exterior windows and doors being locked. The acrid stench of urine was the first to permeate the room. This was not the smell of a toilet not having been flushed for a while. The acrid fumes were unbearable and attempts to stay in the room were short lived and we always found ourselves taking refuge outside. If this indeed was urine then it was an age old build up unlike that of a modern drainage problem. No sooner would the overwhelming eye watering stench appear than it would recede, leaving no trace of its origins.

A second odour which was very distinct was the unmistaken smell of 'wet dog'. Nothing I have found can replicate this distinctive pungent smell and as far as I have researched, dogs had not been the pets of choice for the Pritchard family.

The third odour encountered was by far the worst. The stench of human excrement occasionally filled the small living room and hallway. This was one thing I could not stomach and always took refuge outside until the air cleared.

We had been told by one local resident the smell of canon fire was commonplace around and within the house. For me this would have been phenomena I could explain. The nearby Castle was impregnable and Oliver Cromwell desperately needed to breach the thick stone walls. Nevison, Baghill and Chequerfield were transformed into a series of artillery barrages whose aim was to pulverise the walls in readiness for a breach by foot soldiers. If there was a residual haunting then gunfire smoke would be a good candidate for permeating the area with tragic effects from the past. Unfortunately the cannons evaded us and none of our visits ended in a crescendo of volley shots from the town's sieges.

Each visit always ended on a high as different phenomena was offered every time. Only the bangs and knocks were consistent with each stay and nothing now surprised us. The only real disappointment was that we never physically witnessed anything being moved in the house. Objects moved but always out of eye and camera shot. Sceptics will naturally dismiss eyewitness testimony without evidence to support claims of something others reported to have happened. I accept this so any experience not actually captured on camera I always lay down with caution. The bible on our very first visit to the house had moved without any doubt.

Unfortunately photographs are open to question to those not present. The aim of this book, as I have already said, is simply to try and uncover the truth of a story spanning generations.

If there had been Poltergeist activity I suspect for whatever reason this had subsided long ago. The energy from whatever source arrived, caused terror and simply burnt out like any portable power supply. The energy of 'Fred' came and went, recorded for prosperity in just a few published works. How could this be true? A force so strong capable of dragging a young girl up the stairs had simply closed the door and left the house in peace.

To this day nobody on any visit to the house with me has witnessed at first hand objects being moved. Static cameras on sturdy tripods have been dislodged to the floor but without back up cameras to film what had caused this, footage had to be discarded.

I have stated before and will do so again. I am not a paranormal investigator or ghost hunter. Naivety and innocence fuelled my quest when I first visited 30 East Drive. I expected much but was given little. It was this little however which drew me back to the house. Wherever possible I would invite witnesses not connected to me. Friends of friends, often came along simply interested in visiting the house and taking in the atmosphere. None were ghost hunters or paranormal investigators and, in the main, were in fact sceptical. However, each and every one of them experienced happenings, they could not explain. Some reported hearing voices, some seeing shadows flicker across their field of vision and some reported feelings of being pushed from behind as they made their way around the house. Afterwards, these Guests reported having recurrent dreams, focused on the house. Thankfully none of these were negative in nature and seemed to have a common theme of being in the house surrounded by a constant stream of people passing by.

During the investigation we mixed our visits, alternating the times we were there. Darkness increases the fear factor but I doubt this has much bearing on spiritual activity.

The house was still full of intrigue, despite sunlight cascading through the windows. The game of cat and mouse continued, with the same footsteps, bangs and growls we had heard in the darkness.

On one such visit I was simply trying out a new camera, testing out its capabilities on various settings. One series of photographs immediately caught my eye when playing back the footage later that day at home. I had seemingly captured Glynn relaxing on a seat in the corner of the living room, immediately in front of the internal glazed double doors. One photograph depicts what looks like the figure of someone sitting on the reclining chair through the glass. The silhouette looks to be a man, with arms aloft, as if reading a broadsheet newspaper. The image reminded me of Sunday mornings when the man of the house would relax in his favourite chair, perusing the week's news, whist waiting to get ready for a few pre-dinner pints at the local club.

Was it possible the photograph had captured a scene

from the past? East Drive was a puzzle and held its secrets tightly. A never ending maze of questions, yet to be answered.

During one visit we set a camcorder focusing on the china cabinet in the living room. Other visitors had reported the door opening without human contact. Glynn and Gill seated themselves on the settee whilst myself and Sasha took up residence in what had once been Philip's bedroom upstairs. About thirty minutes elapsed without any activity before Glynn shouted me to come downstairs. The cabinet door was wide open and the video camera lay on its side on the carpeted floor.

My initial suspicions were that the camera had dislodged from the tripod and its falling weight on the floor had triggered the magnetic catch on the door, allowing it to open. Thankfully despite the impact the camera remained functional and play back was impressive. The door clearly opens seconds before the camera crashes to the floor ruling out impact as being the cause. What is more startling is how the camera falls. Mounted on a rigid, well balanced mini-tripod it appears to be violently pushed over from its static position. Had we in fact collected video evidence of what other people had witnessed on their own visits to the house?

Whatever information these witnesses held was from their own research before the visit. Thankfully in most cases it was drawn from watching the film. For me this was advantageous. I avoided taking known friends or associates along with me. Friendship can lead to collusion and I was desperate to avoid this at all cost. I knew more and more as the book progressed I would be under scrutiny from sceptics and those who simply thought they knew better from their own limited knowledge of the house and its history. Everyone joining me had to be independent in their beliefs and ready to challenge and be challenged with any evidence collected.

Early experiments with the ghost box gave seemingly positive results. Trial and error sessions were conducted over a period of weeks and we soon found the best results were recorded in a reverse sweep of FM channels at high speed.

Glynn was even worse than me when it came to technology. In his early days of paranormal investigation more was relied on the sensitive side of the mind rather than scientific apparatus. After spending probably twenty minutes explaining how the spirit box works I turned the switch on. Instantly a women's voice came through the speaker eerily asking 'Do you want to talk with us?' To be honest this took us by complete surprise and the rest of the day was spent with repeated playback of what had been recorded.

Most of the recordings would be dismissed as bleed over from radio broadcasts but some seemed genuine. Direct questions were asked with a thirty second delay for any possible answer. Names repeated were Michael, Philip and Elsbeth. Michael was interesting as the story of the Black Monk related to Father Michael, 'Fred' as he was infamously known locally.

Father Michael still troubled me. It was widespread in the 1600's (when the vile act of child murder had supposedly been committed) monks were referred to as brothers. Father tends to refer to a priest within the upper echelons of a monastery's chain of command.

If indeed a rogue monk had committed an act of paedophilia and murder then perhaps, to save religious face the story could have been covered up. If a Father were to commit such a vile crime then surely this would, if not kept secret, be recorded within the dark annals of history and folklore.

'Fred' I now believed was not a man of the cloth at all. For over forty years the Black Monk reigned supreme without anyone challenging the validity of the story. He had seemingly terrorised a family into almost submission, sparked media interest and carried on his story decades later with the movie 'When the Lights Went Out.'

My suspicions grew. Ghost box sessions continued over the next two months with some success. I was still plagued with rogue radio interference polluting the recordings. However, there was an answer. Paranormal groups had for several years faced the same problem. Slowly I realised that to gain accurate results from the recordings then all but direct answers to specific questions should be treated with caution for validity.

At first our EVP sessions were basic with simple questions. We would ask if there were spirits within the house, how many and their names.

The answers were promising both in real time and recorded playback. Each portion of the recordings were time and date stamped for reference and I found a useful online audio editing programme which was relatively easy to use with a little practice and patience.

The software allowed cropping, speed control and more importantly a feature which enabled background noise to be removed enabling captured voices to be heard more clearly.

Despite our first recordings being amateurish and using trial and error we did accumulate a striking pattern of results. The number eight repeated itself over and over whenever we asked how many were present with us in the room. Names re-occurred during each and every session and it seemed that if were indeed making contact with spirits, it was the same energy coming through on a regular basis. The names 'Michael', 'Elspeth', 'Simon' and 'Fred' came through during each recording.

Michael was no surprise after all he was allegedly the main player to the story. Elspeth and Simon were unknown connections 'Fred' however needed no introductions. Mister Nobody and later Fred were names used by the Pritchard family whenever activity happened within the house.

Father Michael appears, I suspect much later, when a medium allegedly made contact with whatever occupied the house. The whole story centred itself on one individual haunting, but now it seemed numerous entities were to be found within the house. The family only ever made reference to one spirit, or poltergeist, but now, however, this has seemingly expanded into a haunting on a much broader scale.

Why had others investigating the story simply focused on 'Fred' as being the sole culprit? Had they missed vital evidence or had other spirits been brought into the house by those caught up with the sightseeing tours, following the film's release? If indeed this was the case then I suspect the Black Monk of Pontefract was happy with his new found company and rejoices today in the attraction the story continues to create.

If 'Fred' had been real at all he was now quite vocal. EVP recordings suggested he was not one to avoid the use of obscenities and foul language in his spiritual replies.

Later playback from the recordings clearly indicated any answers had to be taken with a pinch of salt. The energy responding to set questions was both a liar and deceiver.

During one recording it was asked how many spirits were in the house. 'Six' was the immediate reply followed seconds later by 'ten, you fucker.'

Often the spirit would give his name as 'Michael,' then seconds later the answer would be 'Got you, it's Fred.'

Despite deviousness of truth one thing did remain constant. Whatever occupied the house seemed to have a hatred for anything connected to the Catholic Church. I, personally, am not a religious man, but I never cast my own opinions onto the beliefs of others. It is my standing that religion deserves respect but East Drive offered none whenever faced with Catholicism. EVP sessions were full of obscenities and mockery whenever someone of the faith attempted to voice their religious views.

Steve had given out his religious thoughts to the house during our early stays and this was met with misfortune to say the least. He reported strange knockings at his front door, always in a sequence of three only to find no one was there.

During one shopping day at the local supermarket his wife bought a dozen eggs. Checking, as we do, none of the eggs were broken she proceeded to the checkout only to be met by the horrified cashier, covering her face with a handkerchief. Not only were the eggs broken but each and every one of them was rancid.

During this time I found myself the target of something I could not identify or answer. We decided a 'smart' television was the way forward to move ourselves into the technological world of today. The extra viewing capabilities were fantastic whilst they lasted. Unfortunately all was lost within a week. The television died and could offer no more entertainment to its audience. This was repeated five times spanning a short period of five weeks. Each television was a different brand and was supplied by three separate stores. The electricity supply within the house was checked for irregularities but none were found.

Not long after Steve unfortunately dropped out of the investigation due to other commitments.

With Catholic influence gone my own television viewing mysteriously returned to normal and I could once again flick from Coronation Street to Murder Mysteries on Channel 68.

Interestingly eye witness accounts, if they are to be believed say that a Catholic Priest entered the house in the early 1970's intent to cleanse whatever presence was haunting there. Apparently he left the house more quickly than he had entered vowing never to return. Unfortunately the story seemed lost to truth and accuracy as with the passing of time those involved had passed away or turned their backs on the property, forever.

We found whenever religious views or opinions entered into conversation we received aggressive EVP responses. Respect seemed to be the key. Confrontation was met with negativity and mirrored responses. In life there is a saying 'behaviour breeds behaviour'. In simple terms it means if you meet someone and smile a friendly greeting then this in most cases will be given back in response.

Strange maybe I know, but I now believe the spirit world is no different in this instance to that of our own. Show respect and this will be reflected back.

This was highlighted in one of the EVP sessions conducted in the presence of two mediums, Phil Bates and Mandy Welton. The recordings were taken at 11.30pm in the bedroom which had once been that of Philip Pritchard's. Despite being sat in darkness, within minutes a shadow made itself known to the mediums in the open doorway overlooking the staircase.

Unfortunately at this stage I had no infra-red equipment and the night vision camcorder only penetrated the darkness at one lux. This meant to work efficiently there would have to be the same lighting as that generated by one candle.

Despite not being able to distinguish any shadow in the darkness I blindly thumbed my way through my well rehearsed control sequences of the spirit box and digital recorder and placed both on the bed beside Phil and Mandy. The responses for the next forty minutes were unbelievable.

Who's at the door? (Mandy)
Somebody, go bollocks
Will you have your photograph taken? (Mandy)
No photograph
Will you let us help you? (Mandy)
Please, he's here. It's Michael
Is it Michael, Father Michael or Brother Michael? (Mandy)
Fred....Contact
We are trying to find out the truth, will you let us? (Mandy)
Please....He's here
Whose here? (Mandy)
Michael
Did you say Michael? (Mandy)
No....George
Is it Michael, Father Michael or Brother Michael? (Mandy)
Fred

Is it brother as in monk or sibling? (Mandy)
Sibling
Did you say sibling? (Mandy)
Yes I did
Does the monk piss you off? (Mandy)
Glory seeking fuck....What's your question?
Do you not want to speak with Philip? (Mandy)
Prick
What is your problem Michael? (Phil)
I speak.....leave
Are you a liar Michael? (Phil)
Why? I've a lady
Is she there because she wants to be there or are you holding her? (Phil)
Holding her
Why are you holding her? (Mandy)
Cos I must....evil. She's evil
I apologise. Is it her that's evil? Are all women evil? (Mandy)
Bitch!
Will you move the curtain? (Mandy)
Why?
Come on Michael is this the best you can do? You're a coward. (Phil)
Dickhead
Come on Michael. (Phil)
I challenge
Do you challenge my guides Michael or are you a coward? Maybe you are a child molesting coward. (Phil)
More people....(Child laughs)

Do you have a child with you? (Mandy)
No
What do you want to achieve? (Mandy)
Shut up bitch

Unfortunately at this point batteries in both the spirit box and digital recorder failed. Despite being of a high quality brand and brand new they had lasted less than thirty minutes. Not to be outdone I quickly retrieved fresh batteries from downstairs and the session was continued.

Are you still here? (Mandy)
Certainly, he's with me
Who's with you? (Mandy)
Brother
Can you rock the bed? (Mandy)
Don't want to, I hold back
Will you have a photograph with me? (Mandy)
No photograph
Can you rock the bed? (Mandy)
I hold back
Have you a message for me please? (Mandy)
You're a dick.....big dick
Do you want the truth to come out or do we keep giving the fame to the Black Monk of Pontefract? (Mandy)
Please
Do you want the truth to come out? (Mandy)
What you gonna do about it? I like to push/touch people

Are you wanting us to bring out the truth? (Mandy)
You're psychic
Could you tell me please how many girls were murdered? (Mandy)
Eight
Could you tell us their names please? (Mandy)
Gives eight syllables in a row. *That's it*
Why were they murdered? (Mandy)
Seven Sexual….Mi brother
So was it your brother? (Mandy)
He did this my brother
Did you get set up? (Mandy)
I did
What's your brother's name? (Mandy)
Simon, Simon
Can we have your permission that Phil can speak? with you? (Mandy)
Yes
Michael I understand will you please open up? (Phil)
Yes
Do you want the hauntings to cease? (Phil)
I'm stuck
Would a blessing help you? (Phil)
Maybe
Do you want peace? (Phil)
I live with that…… Mind your back
Is that a threat? (Phil)
No promise
Are you confident I know the truth? (Phil)
Shoot me

Have you anything more to say? (Phil)
Through you?
Through me yes. (Phil)
Yes
Do you like people to visit this house? (Phil)
Get them out

Unfortunately the batteries once again drained and allowed any further communication to cease. Despite being just into the early hours we decided to end the night on a high. We had recorded intelligent answers to questions asked and without battery power continued questions were useless without documented response.

Before finally leaving we collectively soaked up the atmosphere immediately outside 30 East Drive. The circular grassed roundabout was raised and with imagination this would have once been an elevated position overlooking the ancient town below. The sprawling council estate now hides away the importance of Chequerfield as a once strategic stronghold of the Roundheads as they laid siege to the Royalist garrison below. Take away the red tiled roofs of the houses and look towards the castle and anyone can easily get a true feel of the Chequerfield which once was.

If anyone wants to take in the atmosphere of the house they should first take a slow tour by car of the entire estate at night. Daylight hours offer a busy place, people going about their daily business and driving instructors making use of the mini town layout of roundabouts and countless junctions. The early hours offer something very different. After each visit I always gave thought to the other tenants and home owners of the estate. How many had experienced things they could never fully explain but were wary of telling others in fear of being ridiculed just as the Pritchard family had suffered all those years ago.

Chapter Eight
Fact from Fiction

September saw a shift in the investigation as I sifted my way slowly through hundreds of photographs and countless hours of both audio and video footage. Ninety five percentage of recorded material was discarded and only what could not be explained was saved.

I was now also experiencing recurrent dreams of my own which centred primarily in the house. Each and every night I was sat on the sofa seemingly playing host to a never ending procession of people walking slowly from the staircase to the kitchen. As one figure diminished another took its place in the queue. Dreams like this continue to this day and I have been reassured this is quite normal when delving into the spirit world.

Another thing bothered me now as I painstakingly sifted through everything recorded. 'Fred' was referred to both as being a malevolent spirit of a long dead monk and also a poltergeist. If the poltergeist had the force to throw objects and furniture across rooms, drag a young girl upstairs where had this now gone? We had found objects moved during our stays but these were usually paper cards and coins set as trigger objects. Could such a force simply appear and vanish leaving only a very remnant of what it once was? I suspected the poltergeist activity and the monk were in fact very separate entities.

Historical records relate to the area immediately adjoining what is now East Drive as being worked by monks dating back to 1314.

One such record states 'I, William de Aula, son of Richard of Pontefract have confirmed to the monks there serving God with my body, for the good of my soul and of all my ancestors and heirs, a plot of five acres of land in the fields of Pontefract which is called Flaghill.'

Flaghill on a later map of the early 1800's shows a boundary dividing modern day East Drive towards what is now known as Baghill.

This piece of evidence came as no surprise. Pontefract had been the home of several priories one of which had recently been excavated beneath the foundations of the demolished general hospital nearby.

Monks were etched into the fabric of the area and so it would be no surprise if any haunting should be attributed to long lost souls of a religious order. Again, however, I was constantly drawn back to historical fact. If indeed a monk was guilty of child rape and murder this would have become embedded in history and folklore. The church may be capable of many things but gossip and hearsay always prevails through time and memory. For me this was a huge disappointment. I had grown up with the story of a crazed monk terrorising a local family and memories of schoolyard tales of horror were now debunked. Not to take the whole story away from the monk I do believe now there is a spirit within the house which relates to a presence of the nearby friary but in no way is this guilty of happenings either now or back to the original hauntings.

'Fred' was also a mystery. In the book 'Poltergeist' Colin Wilson records the Pritchard family initially referring to the poltergeist as 'Mr Nobody'. When the haunting reoccurred in 1974 the name had been switched to 'Fred'.

I was aged nine at the time and still vividly remember the ghostly spirit which festered in each and every dark recess amongst the night time streets of the local area. Mother's warned us to be home by a certain time and if we disobeyed this then the 'Bogey Man' would snatch us away forever. Why then the name 'Fred' when local tradition had already labelled and installed a ghostly figure into the local community. Not one to let something go without research I scoured the records for any person remotely connected to the name being executed by hanging. After several hours I was excited with the search results. Historically there had been a Fred from Pontefract who was hanged, not for the crime of child rape and murder but for treason. Forgive my repetition at this stage but I must stress again the following.

'Frederick de Alcyonius (47) Native of Pontefract Saturday 28th March 1587.

Hanged, beheaded and quartered at St. Leonard's, Green Dykes, without Walmgate Bar. The unfortunate culprit was drawn from the castle of York upon a sledge to the fatal spot, where he suffered the severe penalty of the law. Since his condemnation his behaviour had been such as became his unhappy situation, and he acknowledged the justice of his sentence.

After the execution he was beheaded, quartered; his head was set on Walmgate Bar, with his quarters. This execution took place at three o'clock in the afternoon, in the presence of not less than 8,000 spectators.

This was a traitor's death and indeed it is stated in York and York Castle by A.W.Twyford that the crime for which he were executed was petty treason'. (Unfortunately, the records of the North-Eastern Assize circuit for the Tudor period do not survive, so we have no further particulars, but petty treason could include the murder of a master by his servant).

Was this indeed 'Fred?' Unfortunately this was a question to which I had no answer. Frederick de Alcyonius was recorded as living at Pontefract but I have found no further records to expand on who he was and more importantly where he had once lived in the town. I am not a historian and invite those of the profession to seek out records of Frederick. If anyone can connect the name to modern day East Drive this would be a bonus. If not 'Fred' remains a mystery.

More interestingly I found a hand drawn map of Chequerfield dated about 1820 which recorded a monument for the battle of Waterloo. The monument was installed on Chequerfield Circle in September 1818, by the then Mayor of Pontefract Edward Trueman. Unfortunately this historic landmark was demolished following world war two to make way for the new council estate.

I traced the modern day location of what is now 30 East Drive to an area on the map labelled Gill Croft. On the hand drawn map the enclosure is shown as being a large area of land occupied by an orchard. Incidentally, the name Chequerfield is derived from the tree Sorbus Torminalis, otherwise known as the 'wild service tree' or 'chequer tree' due to the pattern of its fruit, which must have grown abundantly there at some time past.

To the orchard's boundary facing Pontefract lay the area of Flaghill and to its Carlton flank was the enclosure known as Bendle Hedge. Both these enclosures are recorded as being worked by the monks of the local priories.

The question of a monk connection to the property cannot be disputed neither can the residual energies of the countless soldiers who died at the battle centuries ago.

Without historical evidence it is impossible to point the finger of blame for the original hauntings to one long dead individual. It would be a nice romantic end to finally attribute the haunting to a monk wrongly hanged for a crime he did not commit being resurrected in the spirit realm to punish those now living on the land he once knew. Unfortunately this for me was not to be. I soon suspected the story of the Black Monk was far more complex than anyone had ever imagined. Back in the 1960's and early 1970's it was easier to speculate and impress your opinions onto others. Historical research was painstakingly slow with only paper documents having to be traced and scrutinised. Any evidence either factual or presumed was easier to sell to an audience in need of explanation and understanding without the risk of being ridiculed and questioned. Thankfully today is very different. The internet gives everyone the chance to be an expert in any subject they desire. Genealogy and local history are open networks to those wishing to trace a specific name or event and it is now far easier for anyone to conduct research or question the research carried out by others.

Despite being over forty years since the Black Monk first hit the headlines I am surprised not one full investigation has been conducted to establish the truth. As I pen my own experiences about East Drive I am preparing for a backlash from sceptics, those who feel they have a better explanation and others who simply wish to keep the story of the Black Monk alive. My own story is different.

Surprisingly local views on the haunting are hard to find. Times move and most residents have long since moved on or died leaving a younger generation to keep the housing estate alive. Those remaining who know the story seem to keep its history private. The few who do break the mysterious code of silence fall into two categories. One camp is pro poltergeist and the other claim the story as being that of nonsense, made up by the Pritchard family to gain a financial outcome. My position obviously is based on the former. I have been unable as yet to uncover any monetary gain by the family made either during the original haunting or media coverage afterwards.

Chapter Nine
When the Lights Go Out

With each visit to East Drive we never once came away disappointed. Those thinking only the hours of darkness opened up gateways to the spirit world are quite wrong in their beliefs. Within the walls we found activity to be present both during the heat of the summer's sun and beneath the crescent moon.

Darkness adds to the fear factor. Whatever cannot be seen in the darkened shadows triggers our inbuilt mechanism of flight or fight. Most of us unfortunately visit cemeteries to lay flowers in remembrance of loved ones lost. During the day these places can offer solace and comfort to cushion bereavement. Visit the same place however during the hours of darkness and the cemetery becomes a very different place indeed. The comfort zone withdraws as the shadows lengthen and the same environment changes from a place of serenity to one of fear.

East Drive was different. Despite the well repeated story of the evil monk, for me, the property never presented as being influenced by evil or any entity intent on causing harm to human visitors. Unexplained happenings remained constant whatever the hour. Experiences we had during the day were met with simply intrigue. I had been wrong. Daylight offered little escape from activity other than the ebbing back of the shadows and giving comfort to those harbouring an inner fear of the dark. Unfortunately, it seems a common belief that paranormal activity only occurs at night. We soon found this to be both inaccurate and misguided. One particular summer's afternoon gave testimony to this, as both Glynn and I spent a couple of hours at the house. With bright sunlight bathing the interior of the building we decided to follow our own intuitions and separated, seeking out areas of the house which gave us personal reasons to investigate. Glynn chose the parents' bedroom and for some reason I decided on the smallest room which had been the daughter's. Despite the original story being centred on this particular room, for us, this was a part of the house which until now had offered the least activity. The single bed lay lopsided against the wall, two of its wooden legs allegedly being broken by the poltergeist months before our first visit, a recent occurrence, and the 1970's polystyrene ceiling tiles bore scars as if once falling prey to being bombarded with solid objects.

Taking comfort from the latest flare up of sciatica I knelt down, resting my elbows on the bed. Foolish bravery overcame me and I vocally aired my opinion that anyone capable of harming a child was both monstrous and void of human compassion. The response to my outburst shook me to the core. Immediately the bed lifted, perhaps six centimetres off the floor, before banging back down onto the patched-up carpet. All hint of manly bravado left me in an instant and without realising, I cried out for assistance. Glynn came charging in and finding a quivering wreck, assisted me down the stairs.

Once downstairs, we discussed and explored every explanation of how a wooden frame could rise up from the floor with almost the full weight of a grown man, pressing it down. What gave us more concern was the fact this had happened in direct response to a statement of confrontation and disdain.

'Fred' it now seemed could not only comprehended our modern language and its nuances but was also more than capable of using force and strength, despite the passing of years since he revelled in his finest hour. Time holds no sway within East Drive. The same experiences encountered in darkness offered a very different response. For me it is this fear factor which plays a dominant role at East Drive. Perhaps it was this that had originally played a role in the first recorded hauntings of the Pritchard family. Fear and imagination whenever mixed, creates a potent brew difficult to swallow and I suspect this played some part in the hype when 'Fred' first appeared.

I would never question the family's testimony to events they claimed to have happened. During my own research for the book I admit I was tempted many times to trace the remaining Pritchard's but respect for their privacy was at the forefront of my own eager quest for the truth. This book is not concerned with happenings from the past but focuses on what remains today.

East Drive today is but a remnant of what it once was. Any violent force has thankfully ebbed back into the shadows from which it had once emerged. In my opinion 'Fred' simply burnt out. Whatever energy had been created allowing the spirit to manifest fully was spent and only the dying embers remained for the next forty years.

The story of the Black Monk is slowly becoming lost in time. Today's children, unfortunately in my opinion, have little, if any, interest in times past and submerse themselves in the never ending advancements of technology. Long gone are the days of hanging around dark street corners having harmless fun and re-kindling stories from folklore and tradition to keep heritage alive.

Computers games and mobile technology have filled the void. Age old stories are becoming lost to the new generations and the story of the poltergeist was just a distant memory for the ageing and diminishing local inhabitants who witnessed first-hand just what the Pritchard family witnessed. The Black Monk it seemed had taken his last bow, gracefully, to the curtain call. The audience of believers was gone and there was no reason for the manifestation to continue.

Time moves on regardless and the once thriving family house fell silent. Mr Pritchard sadly passed away and the two children reached an age where they left the family nest to seek out their own lives and destinies. Jean Pritchard remained however until the three bed roomed house simply out grew her capabilities of husbandry and management. Pride gave way to reality and she eventually moved into a sheltered housing complex nearby.

With the Pritchard family gone this could have been the end to the story. Shortly after the house became empty it was purchased by an unlikely source. Stories of the Poltergeist it seemed had reached London and plans were made to make a film of the haunting. 'Fred' finally, it seemed, had got the audience he desired.

The film was aired to audiences across the United Kingdom and was met with a new found interest in the house. Public interest once again grew and the Poltergeist was resurrected into the annals of local history.

Movie goers flocked in vast numbers to view the house and tours were conducted, with a small gate fee, to help with the maintenance costs of the property. Slowly as memories of the film reduced so, too, did the crowds.

I watched the film at the local cinema soon after its release. Artistic licence was evident throughout the movies duration and I was disappointed filming had not in fact taken place in Pontefract and the family was portrayed missing the actual son. The main part again was played by the evil Cluniac Monk, torn against righteousness to fulfil his own inner perverted desire to have sex and kill a young girl. For me this was nonsense and lacked any historical validity.

There is and never was a demonic monk intent on wreaking havoc at East Drive or any other property on the Chequerfield Estate. The house was and continues to be haunted but in my opinion this is the result of a collection of spirits tied for whatever reason to the area. The spirits which visit the house also roam the surrounding land and I am now convinced this house was highlighted by a family confident enough to face the backlash of ridicule which was always going to arise within a tight knit mining community. I am now sure many of the houses on the estate do have activity the owners and tenants never disclose. The gateway remains within the ground and somehow 30 East Drive appears to be the epicentre of what the local people continue to ignore or at least don't speak openly about.

What continues to puzzle me is why the activity suddenly started almost twenty years after the house was built. The whole estate was built after World War two to replace the back to back slums which surrounded the elevated position of farmland which the estate now occupies. During my research I have been informed 30 East Drive and the attached property next door were the final two houses to be built during this particular phase of development. Locals recall construction seemed to take forever as both houses were targeted by thieves who took advantage of free bricks, timber and other building supplies. This however was almost two decades before the original poltergeist activity began. Unfortunately I have not uncovered any event which could be connected to the first disturbances at the property in the late 1960's. Despite family members being alive I respect their privacy and never, during this investigation sought them out for information. I believe they would have stepped forward to give their own story when the movie was released if they had wanted to.

The second period of activity in 1974 for me was very different. Witnesses were willing to come forward and offer their own personal recollections of what they had witnessed. This was not second hand information and proved invaluable in my own search for the truth.

Phil Bates had already verified the existence of a capped off well situated between both adjoining properties. Phil had also been a life-long friend of Darren who was born next door to the house and continues to live there today. Ironically it was Phil's late father who took on the tedious job of repairing the grandmother clock which it was said had been thrown down the stairs by the poltergeist.

Phil recalls some sort of alteration or building work was being carried out when the hauntings began. Unfortunately this has not been verified other than from memory but it does give credence to disturbance of the land or property which could have opened something allowing paranormal activity to commence.

If it was building work at the house which triggered any activity why then did this not start when the original construction work commenced? Modern foundations for houses are deep and intrusive to the surrounding land and if it was groundwork disturbance why then did the activity not occur when the house was built?

In my opinion, and it is purely my opinion, something happened within the house to provoke whatever was responsible for the original hauntings. I now suspect perhaps the children, in innocence, had somehow opened up a gateway allowing something to cross over into the physical realm. Did they perhaps unwittingly experiment with the Ouija Board or some other form of paranormal communication? Something had occurred without doubt at the property to allow spiritual intrusion into the physical world. Colin Wilson in his book laid blame to puberty and mixed emotions this volatile age can produce. This could be attributed to both hauntings in 1968 and 1974 but has to be discarded for today's continued activity. I have no evidence to suggest major building work was carried out at the property which could have triggered some sort of activity.

Further research found the existence of a documented well in the area. This map is dated 1820 and like the other one hand drawn. The document depicts an oblong structure beside which is written the word 'pump'. Could this be the same well now converted to hand drawn water pulling as was common in the nineteenth century? This reinforces my belief the Black Monk is a myth. There are no records of gallows placed at the area near to East Drive. Gallows Hill is in fact two miles away between the border of Castleford and Pontefract.

If a monk was hanged and finally thrown into the unseen depths of a well what would this achieve? Digging wells meant labour and expertise. Contamination would be avoided at all cost and a corpse would certainly prove the well unfit for use.

If the well was part of a private structure, not open to the public then such contamination would mean the household was void of fresh water. Even in the middle ages no family would allow their water supply to be contaminated with a corpse. This reinforces my belief that the well belonged to the perpetrator of the hideous crime of child murder. To kill the beast of a man would have been satisfying. To throw his dead or dying body into his own water source would be the final nail in the coffin of closure and in some a further act of revenge.

Historically that is about as far as my own research has uncovered. I had hoped to find evidence to support the Black Monk story. I thought this would be an easy task with today's historical fingerprint being open to the masses online. Nothing however is recorded about a monk being executed at Pontefract and even if had been the case and the story covered up by the church, such an event would have been embedded into local legend and folklore.

For me the property was shrouded within a dense blanket of both fact, imagination and fiction. I wanted the story to be true but I had not recorded anything remotely connected to eye witness accounts of the original hauntings. In all my visits to the house I had never felt threatened nor had I witnessed objects being moved to verify poltergeist activity. As with the bible on our first visit it was obvious that some unexplained phenomena was capable of shifting items around the house. Unfortunately this always avoided exposure on recorded playback.

My research, despite continued enthusiasm came to a dead end and no further progress could be made. Each visit to house yielded proof of unexplained activity but most of this was only supported by personal experiences to myself and those who accompanied me on any particular visit. Hearsay and opinion can never be used as evidence and I knew if I were to move my own story of East Drive forward, I would need watertight evidence to substantiate my experiences within the property.

By now I was convinced the house remained haunted. I had witnessed many things which, to this day, I cannot explain. Armed with a portable projector and screen I could happily have given after dinner speeches on my views on the haunting. Personal experiences and opinions, however, can never be set in stone and remain simply stories for amusement. I was now desperate for evidence I could portray other than activity simply witnessed by myself and Glynn. Deep down I knew I required help.

Despite earlier optimism about my equipment purchases I now felt like an ill equipped traveller on a trek to the polar icecap. What I had was good but not adequate enough to make the journey complete. Initial excitement of being part of the house and story was subsiding. Unexplained footsteps and bangs were inconclusive if not supported by recorded proof to quell the tide of sceptics who would inevitably pounce at every opportunity. If my journey into the unknown was to advance I would again have to dig deep into a financial pocket which unfortunately was not bottomless.

As with anything else in today's online marketplace there is an endless supply of scrupulous dealers ready to take advantage of the faceless transaction the internet offers. Unfortunately I found to my cost paranormal research has become a magnet for individuals and companies ready to home in and take advantage of those innocent enough to fall for the promise of quality equipment which will help in scientific research of the unknown. Enthusiasm once again got the better of me and I ordered equipment from several online suppliers. I waited patiently and was disappointed to say the least when the products arrived. It was obvious exploitation was being exercised and scrupulous dealers were cashing in on those, like me, who were attempting to seek out proof of paranormal existence. Trading standards have yet to break into the world of spirit and would have their work cut out sorting through the endless suppliers and distributors of equipment which was not fit for the purpose it was claimed.

Thankfully, just as disillusionment set in, I was given a breakthrough. A paranormal research team had visited East Drive on several occasions and its founder member Glen Smith was beginning to make a name for himself converting standard digital cameras to infra-red.

By the time I made contact Glen had expanded his experience and was producing, made-to-order, research equipment which seemed to have, overall, positive feedback from paranormal groups across the country.

My first two purchases arrived with a week of ordering them. The Panasonic Lumux digital camera was compact and easy to operate even in darkness. The infra-red illuminator was compact and once fitted to the camera looked both professional and fit for the purpose it was designed for. The week ahead saw me almost revert back to my childhood days. My new toy was put to use each and every night within the confines of my own home and garden. No evidence of paranormal activity was collected but my wife, Michelle, and granddaughter, Ava, did make excellent still life models in zero light.

Confidence once again rose within me and armed with the ability to see in total darkness, I impatiently counted down the days to the next visit to the house.

Chapter Ten
Next Steps into the Abyss

So impressed with the converted camera I again contacted Paratech UK and purchased an array of equipment. Photographic evidence can easily be manipulated and accusers will always use this to ridicule and dismiss whatever static material you offer. Video however is more difficult to dismiss so I purchased a converted JVC Everio camcorder with built in memory of 60 gigabytes.

Other purchases included the 'Gotcha' EVP device. This is a great piece of kit especially when used in conjunction with a standard digital recorder. When the audio recorder microphone detects a voice or noise you get a visual confirmation which enables you to see when EVP's or noises you cannot hear occur and you can then 'tag' your audio vocally and video the activity using your camcorder.

Next was to be the 'Shadow/Motion Detector'. This device uses ultrasonic frequencies to detect movement within the investigation area. The range of the units sensors are approximately three meters. An audible alarm is created when movement is detected; the closer the object is to the device the louder the alarm sounds.

Despite my wallet being empty I acted without hesitation and purchased a REM Pod. A mini telescopic antenna is used to detect changes in the magnetic field around the instrument. This field can be easily influenced by materials and objects that conduct electricity. Based on source proximity, strength and electro-magnetic field distortion the unit gives off both audible and visual alarms which increase with the strength and distance created by the source of interference.

Now almost on the breadline I stretched further into poverty and made yet another purchase. Impressed from almost day one with the capabilities of the widely used K11 meter I was immediately drawn to a new addition to the growing array of equipment being made available by Paratech UK. Glen was converting the meters with audible alarms. For me this was the icing on the cake.

For the K11 to be effective in measuring activity it needed either to be placed in an occupied room or have a recording camera focused on the device to record any fluctuation on the sensor's LED lights. With the addition of sound this opened up a whole new dimension to how the K11 could be deployed. For me at this stage of my research this was a must purchase. No longer would I have to deploy a locked down camera to monitor visual readings from the meter. With audio the K11 could be left to its own devices out of sight but within hearing range. With this modification this was a 'must have' purchase for me and any paranormal researcher.

I now felt confident enough to schedule closure to my investigation at East Drive. Despite having collected a lot of evidence to support my own findings, there were in fact unexplainable happenings. I needed now to push this further and finally offer an explanation as to the actual cause. I had not experienced anything to support claims of the Black Monk and I now doubted the story to be true.

Over the next eight weeks my patience and expenditure seemed to finally pay off. I was now able to lock down rooms in total darkness and playback images the following day. Dark shadows were recorded moving across the cameras' viewing lenses. With this movement I also had visual and audio back up with both the K11 meter and REM Pod. Whatever inhabited East Drive was capable of triggering electrical equipment. In real time both the lumux digital camera and JVC Everio camcorder proved invaluable. Still pictures taken in complete darkness show a dark shadow appearing and then disappearing within seconds. Innocently I was taking snaps from the bottom of the stairs upwards. When checked the sequence clearly depicts a black form appearing and suddenly vanishing.

Whilst doing an initial sweep of the house in darkness using only the Everio's screen to offer illuminated guidance I followed and filmed a shadow. The dark figure had to be in front of me as I filmed. The room offered no light and the hand held camera's infra-red illumination was set immediately in front of the lens. Whatever shadow it captured had to be between the wall and lens. I followed the shadow for about thirty seconds before it turned from left to right and disappeared. As always, I did try and replicate this, as I do with all footage, but given the image appeared in front of the infra-red lights and camera I can offer no explanation.

Many hours were spent also taking audio recordings. These in turn were scrutinized carefully using modern software. Most of the voices can be dismissed as passing radio interference. Others simply cannot. Random voices had to be put on hold as these were not evidence to be relied upon. Only direct answers to specific questions could be included in the growing list of evidence we could not explain. Sasha, my daughter, had begun to join us on our visits and for some reason, whenever she used the spirit box, responses would be more often and relevant to the questions being asked. What the reason for this was I do not know. Was she in some way more connected to the spirit world due to her gender and age? For some reason, females and younger females do seem to attract more attention. Why, I have yet to discover.

Still experimenting with the equipment from Paratech UK, I locked down the kitchen area. I mounted the Everio camcorder on a mini tripod and focused the infrared light to cover a Shadow/Motion Detector, K11 meter, REM Pod and EM Pump. This latest edition creates a low level magnetic field in varying pulses and frequencies. It starts out producing .2Hz pulse and increases to 256 Hz pulse. Paranormal investigators claim the pumps can offer energy for spirits to draw upon and materialise.

The equipment was left in total darkness for one hour without human contamination. Elsewhere in the house we sat in relevant silence taking in the atmosphere of the living room. Gill had joined us for the first time.

She was married to Glynn and as well as having a lifelong interest in all things paranormal seemed to have some ability of being sensitive to spiritual activity. Before long Gill picked up a feeling of a young girl singing and skipping-around in the kitchen next door. Overlooking the girl, she sensed, was the presence of a man either protecting the girl or overseeing exactly what she was doing.

Playback of the recording was amazing to say the least. Sixteen minutes in and the shadow detector picked up movement to its right side. The digital readout gave a distance of 0.6 metres. Within a few seconds the reading was gone only to be replaced with the same reading to its left side. This right to left activity reading lasted for six minutes. During this short period the K11 meter detected intermittent high readings accompanied on two occasions by both visual and audible alerts on the Rem Pod.

Could this be energy of the girl Gill had picked up as she danced in circles around the apparatus? Later that evening we set out the equipment in exactly the same way but our second attempt offered no activity on playback.

Later that same evening Gill said she felt childish activity coming from the area immediately in front of the fireplace in the living room. Almost on cue the K11 meter illuminated erratically. If spirits of children were haunting the house could these be attributed to the murders which may have occurred centuries ago?

Activity continued each and every time we visited East Drive. Not one visit however was like the other.

Sometimes it felt the house was seemingly charged with an unseen energy which could be felt immediately on arrival. Dull headaches and feelings of nausea were not uncommon and overwhelming odours of urine and excrement would appear and then dissolve away as if they had never been present.

Other times the interior gave out a sad feeling of emptiness and abandonment. During these times I was taken back to my own childhood memories. August holidays ritually consisted of a two week family holiday at the coast. With the fun gone it always seemed strange to go back home. What was normally a homely and comfortable building, on first entering, would seem empty and our voices would resound like distant echoes between the confines of the walls. This was the same feeling I had at East Drive and on these occasions it felt a sad place to be. Gone were the feelings of uncertainty and trepidation, only to be replaced by those of sadness and perhaps a fall from grace. It felt that whatever energy frequented the building was gone and with its leaving, a void had been created.

During one visit we took a laptop which had Cluniac Monks singing typical hymns from the sixteenth century downloaded onto the hard drive. With all the usual checks done for EMF base readings and photographs taken we pressed the play button and settled ourselves in the living room. A K11 meter was placed in the living room on top of the china cabinet and a REM pod and shadow detector were placed on the floor in the hallway.

Before long the shadow detector and REM pod gave out both visual and audio indications. On closer inspection the REM pod fluctuated rapidly from low to high readings and vice versa which continued for several minutes. The shadow detector constantly recorded movement first from its left side towards the stair case and then to its right. This was repeated over and over again. If indeed the equipment was accurate this indicated something was moving from the bottom of the stairs, over the unit as if to stand at the door and returning to the stairs from where movement was initially detected.

No sooner did activity cease in the hallway the K11 meter flashed into life giving readings in strength from low to high. It seemed whatever was causing the instruments to trigger had paced up and down the hallway before passing through the closed door into the living room. As time passed readings on the K11 meter became sporadic and after perhaps forty five minutes ceased altogether.

Shortly afterwards the final monk sang out his hymn and the downloaded MP3 ended. Despite feelings of excitement the atmosphere within the house again changed to that of emptiness and loss. The once proud family home was merely now a sad shell of what it had once been.

Looking back we should have 'taken the bull by the horns' and utilised the equipment to hand when activity seemed to readily respond to the Cluniac songs. Perhaps we should have used at least the spirit box in an attempt to make contact. Unfortunately we were overcome with the level of activity encountered and for us at the time this had been enough.

Later visits proved fruitless as we tried to recreate the responses using the MP3 recordings. Maybe the entities were not ones to suffer trickery and repetition was simply not their thing.

East Drive remained a puzzle. It was obvious the energy of whatever had plagued the Pritchard family had diminished in strength but given findings from our investigation some lesser form of paranormal activity continues to this day.

The original haunting focused on one entity being solely responsible for the haunting. If this was indeed the case why were we collecting evidence of other spirits occupying the house? From records of the late 1960's and early 1970's there was not one indication of anything other than The Black Monk being responsible for whatever had actually happened.

Chapter Eleven
When the Lights Turned On

For me the search was finally over. By now I had spent well over two thousand hours in the house. Most of this time was spent in darkness but I did also spend time during hours of daylight. Both Steve and I could never have imagined how far the journey would take us as we stepped inside the house on that sunny afternoon which now seemed so long ago. Glynn remained committed to the very end and others including Gill, Glynn's wife and my own daughter, Sasha, had become invaluable as time progressed.

My research had also cost me heavily in financial terms. Each visit ended in me purchasing some sort of equipment in readiness for the next. Early buys often proved unreliable and not fit for the job in hand. This I admit was simply down to my own desire to assemble an array of tools at little cost. Buy cheap buy twice resounded true, and slowly I learnt to dig a little deeper into my pocket if I were to go further in my investigation.

Each and every stay at the house offered something different. Unexplained footsteps and banging noises at this point were everyday occurrences and offered no surprise. Video footage of 'orbs' now outgrew interest if they could not be credited to nothing more than dust particles. In essence the game was finally over. 'Fred, Father Michael and The Black Monk' were now in the dock waiting my personal findings. The trio were charged with causing terror and distress covering a period of over forty years. Now it was time to finally uncover the truth.

The Black Monk perhaps is a myth. Without going into personal detail the haunting had begun with the Pritchard family. Monks were in abundance in history within the area around Pontefract and it would have been easy to lay the blame on a brother somehow fallen from grace. Had the house been situated near to Disney Land then I suspect we could be looking at the spectre of Mickey Mouse himself.

Father Michael is also a non-starter. There was no Father Michael connected in any way to murders on the ground of what is now East Drive. The only connection to a man of the cloth being executed at Chequerfield bares nothing on the story. As for the area known as 'Priest Bridge' this is located about a mile away near to the old hospital.

Putting the story behind me I entered East Drive with an open mind. I wanted 'Fred' to make an appearance and pose before the camera. 'Fred' as he was previously described unfortunately did not appear and so my own search was forced to delve deeper into the mystery.

Where, then, does the story of 30 East Drive lead? Paranormal activity remains in and around the house but thankfully this has subsided in ferocity to that witnessed by the Pritchard family. What had caused so much anger and hatred I can only guess. Had some building work taken place at the property or within its vicinity disturbed something better left in slumber? Had the family innocently summoned something by experimenting in Ouija boards or some other form of spirit contact? Had some entity attached itself to both children as they reached the sometimes troubled times of puberty?

Whatever the reason was for the activity it is obvious when reading documented evidence the family were not dealt with respect and caution by whatever had manifested within the family home.

The haunting was not that of friend but was obviously full of anger and aimed its rage directly at those residing or visiting within the house.

On two separate occasions a family had been subjected to what is now recorded as one of the most violent acts of poltergeist activity in Europe. One occurrence is bad enough for anyone to endure but for the activity to repeat itself six years later is overwhelming to imagine.

What does trouble me however is why the family stayed in the house if something so terrible was happening? The council, as it was called then, was the largest landlord of rentable accommodation in the country. House swaps and exchanges were common practice and a trip to the nearest housing office was all it needed to put your name on a list for consideration.

Strange creaks and groans can simply be attributed to subsidence and structure movement. Chequerfield is built on rich coal reserves which have been mined for over one hundred and fifty years. Coal extraction however and ground subsidence cannot explain what was being reported at East Drive.

With the second account of poltergeist activity gone in 1974 the family continued a normal family life. The children finally fled the nest to seek out their own lives and the mother continued to reside in the house until just a few years ago when she secured a place in a nearby retirement home. A local resident did inform me during the course of my investigation that once left to live in the house alone the mother tended to use the kitchen as her main living quarters and preferred not to spend time in the living room. This of course is information from a third party and has not been verified for the purpose of the book. What is interesting however is the fact the glazed panelled double doors which separate the living room to the kitchen are fitted with a lock. Household locks are usually employed to keep unwanted intruders out of the house. Why then would anyone feel the need to lock off an internal door with the exception perhaps of a toilet and wash room?

There are many questions about 30 East Drive which I fear will never be fully answered. Colin Wilson in his own book 'Poltergeist' I feel missed an opportunity to seek out the root cause of what had actually happened. He had direct access to the family but unfortunately left out vital research which could have reinforced or dismissed credence to the story.

This book was never meant to document or question happenings from a past I had no way of delving into wanting answers. The book is about East Drive as it stands today. I began with an open mind and sat on the fence hoping the story held some truth. I hoped my childhood memories would not be tainted forever with uncovering something which was made up of imagination and lies.

Thankfully from day one this was not to be the case. It now seems a distant memory from the first time I entered the house but the bible had moved, the footsteps overhead were real and chairs were pulled away from their places underneath the table. From that very moment I was convinced there was something beyond my ability to simply shrug away.

Unless recorded correctly, history is something which cannot be used for the purpose of evaluating fact. The book could have been completed simply on what had already been written, eye witness testimony from those who knew the family and hearsay from those connected to the original story. For me this was never what I intended. The truth about the house needed to be told and I feel this could only be achieved through first-hand experience and an open mind.

So what does haunt East Drive? Time spent at the house was also taken up with never ending reading on the subject of hauntings, spirits and paranormal activity.

The Philip experiment I suspect bears no link to happenings at the house. This had been conducted in the confines of a scientific investigation by professionals. I doubt any individual living or visiting East Drive in the 1960's would have been capable of recreating what the scientists had achieved.

I also researched the Stone Tape Theory in the hope this could offer an explanation.

The theory was examined closely in the 1970s as a possible explanation for ghosts and residual hauntings in particular. The Stone Tape Theory speculated inanimate materials could absorb energy from living beings. In other words an invisible recording is laid down during moments of high tension, such as murder or any event which may cause extreme stress in the human mind. This stored energy can subsequently be released, resulting in a display of the recorded activity of what happened in real time. The replay can take the form of a full manifestation or partial sounds such as voices or footsteps. Paranormal investigators commonly refer to such phenomena as residual hauntings. Ghosts are not spirits but non-interactive recordings similar to the registration capacities of an audiotape machine that can playback previously recorded events.

While the theory may explain some ghostly sightings, no one knows what the recorded energy actually is. However, the possibility that it could be composed by our natural electric and magnetic fields is one of the explanations that the Stone Tape Theory advances.

30 East Drive, however, does not fully meet with the theory and its strict criteria alone. Very few accounts relate to any re-enactment being played out from past events other than odours like those of what we would expect from the vicinity of a medieval farmyard.

During my own time spent at the house I have been confronted on many occasions with a presence which is both intelligent and fully aware of the modern day surroundings and more importantly the living. I was never privy to replays of a battle long gone nor have I witnessed hangings of unfortunates, falling foul of our very British and civilised courts of law.

The answer for me lay in the use of the Ouija Board. I suspect someone had experimented without fully comprehending what the consequences could be. Not only do I suspect the board being used by someone connected to the Pritchard family, there is evidence it continues to being used in the house today.

On several occasions we found planchette's which had been left behind by previous visitors to the house. These are small heart-shaped piece of wood or plastic used as a movable indicator to indicate the spirit's message by spelling it out on the board during a séance.

I had, personally and innocently, experimented with the board in my youth as I know many others have. Naivety and enthusiasm unfortunately blocked away the risks. After all the Ouija had originally been marketed and sold simply as a game of amusement. How wrong could I have been? Answers to specific questions had come thick and fast and after just twenty minutes the experience was enough to frighten everyone involved, into making a joint promise never to experiment again. The makeshift board of cardboard and paper hand drawn alphabet were burnt and thankfully the episode was laid to rest.

It does not take a seasoned historian to accept the whole of Chequerfield had been a place of bloodlust and suffering. The very soil of the elevated strategic position has been drenched in blood and gore.

Unfortunately this bloody past has been somewhat lost to the local residents. The nearby castle despite being demolished under direct orders from Oliver Cromwell remains sadly a backseat attraction behind the many public houses and twice weekly market. Cromwell had demolished the castle because of its impregnable defences and he simply had not been able to breach these in the civil war. If the royalist garrison was to rise again he feared this would be their final bastion of defiance which would never be captured.

If anyone wanted to experiment with the Ouija Board then for me East Drive was the place to open whatever doorway the board could offer. Once the doorway was opened I suspect those responsible were not able to seal the connection between the living and spirit world. Any doorway or portal opened by the ignorant to all things paranormal may well have been subject to one way traffic, hence today's continued hauntings.

The idea of Ouija experiment offers credence to paranormal activity at East Drive. In my opinion someone in the 1960's had innocently played along with something they had no concept of and the consequences of their act of amusement had created something they could never have imagined.

The board was created originally as a toy and readily available for public purchase without the need to hunt down shops dedicated to selling paranormal equipment.

In the late 1960's the family's son would have been a child entering early teenage years. In those bygone days children made their own fun along the streets and wooded areas around their homes. Televisions were a rare commodity and games consoles were not even scripted in episodes of even the most imaginative TV shows. Without computers and video games play was left to the devices of imagination and available resources. Had the son and his friends delved into something with childish experimentation? If this was the answer why then did the haunting cease? Could the activity be recreated some eight years later with the daughter experimenting once again with using the Ouija Board as she herself reached puberty?

For me this is too much of a coincidence. If every use of the Ouija Board resulted in poltergeist activity then there would not be any village, town or city without unexplained activity taking place.

As my research finally draws to a close I suspect three separate theories could have combined in some way to create the now infamous Black Monk of Pontefract.

Almost laid to rest after over forty years the film again resurrected the terror experienced by the family and those people closely associated with them.

30 East Drive is a haunted place. My time there has removed all trace of doubt I held immediately before my first visit to the house.

Ghostly tales from my childhood were now for me a reality I could not discard or counteract with logical explanation. So many things had happened during my countless visits for me to simply ignore. Each stay offered activity and what remains puzzling is this activity is never the same. On occasions voices of children had been heard and recorded as EVP's. These stays were usually enhanced with a feeling of childish play and mischief as if a game of hide and seek was being played out. Noises would be heard coming from empty rooms and on investigation the same sounds would be heard coming from the room we had just vacated.

Sessions with the Spirit Box would often produce children's voices. On one occasion Gill said she sensed children dancing in a circular motion in the area that is now the kitchen. Before Gill could finish the sentence the Shadow detector which had been placed on the kitchen floor earlier began to indicate movement first to its right and then left. This continued for about three minutes with the nearby K11 meter also giving intermittent high readings.

On other occasions it was as if adult presences were in the house. These did not feel at all sinister and recordings indicate they were both intelligent and welcoming. Direct answers to questions could often be gained and as long as respect was given they seemed welcoming to our visits.

One session with the spirit box we were provided with proof of an intelligent presence in the house. I had printed A4 sheets of paper with numbers and names prior to our visit. With the spirit box performing a reverse sweep in FM mode the papers were passed individually in front of a camcorder before Sasha asked what each word was written on the paper. Seven out of the ten responses were correct. Each answer, however, was never spoken by just one voice, several voices, all different, seemed to be in competition to be the first one to respond with the right answer, as if taking part in an invisible television quiz show to win the star prize.

Sometimes sweet aromas would fill the rooms and these would leave as quickly as they occurred.

Unfortunately however another presence was all too often encountered. This was not mischievous or welcoming and whenever this entered the house all other activity ceased.

If it was this the Pritchard family had encountered then I feel this would have been a terrifying experience. Growls could often be heard and a dark mass was seen on several occasions both on the staircase and kitchen. This mass was large and we estimated it to stand at almost seven foot tall. This presence was also followed by strong odours. These however were not pleasant and resembled the stench of human excrement, urine and what I can only describe as that of 'wet dog' which all canine lovers will easily associate with.

Could this be the entity which attacked the family on two separate occasions? Each attack had occurred over a period of months and each was both violent and destructive. The perpetrator on both counts was portrayed as being a hooded figure, very tall and black in appearance with no visible face. Could this be the same entity we had experienced first-hand during the many visits to the house?

I note with interest subsequent visitors to the house, prior to the book's release, also report seeing a tall, almost black shadow move across the walls in the living room, kitchen, staircase and the bedrooms.

Was this the same darkness which had appeared as I raced upstairs to silence the motion detector? Despite my upfront bravery on that occasion a deep rooted sense of fear and panic had overwhelmed me and I could do little other than to cower on the staircase, helpless.

The family reported odours similar to those found on a farmyard. Were these the same smells we encountered on occasions when we had to vacate rooms due to acrid odours of urine and excrement made staying in the immediate vicinity impossible?

Documentation from the original activity also accounts objects being moved through solid matter. Tired of eggs being broken on the kitchen floor from the safety of the refrigerator Mrs Pritchard decided to place her breakfast commodities inside a wooden box. The container it seemed was no different and the eggs found their way shattered across the floor. This for me was a story too far-fetched to believe. Solid objects simply do not pass through other solid material without damage.

Disbelief however for me turned into reality on one of my later visits to the house. On this occasion we were seated in the living room in darkness. Doors to the kitchen and hallway were closed and my daughter,

Sasha, was vocally beckoning any spirits to come forward and make contact. Sasha had been a late comer to our vigils and it seemed whenever she joined us activity increased. A sense of inner bravery must have overcome her and she called out for something in the room to be thrown. Almost on cue she let out a scream shouting something had hit her.

On inspection a large button lay immediately in front of her on the carpet. As with all our stays at the house we would immediately take as many photographs in every room for future reference. Several photographs showed the button to have been on the kitchen table on our arrival. It is likely this had been used as a trigger object by someone visiting the house earlier that week. For the button to have been used as a projectile and make physical contact with Sasha then it must have passed through a glazed door without damaging the glass. Could this be associated with the same phenomena as the eggs? I am no scientist and this was far beyond my understanding. Solid objects simply do not move through glass without breakage so now I was truly baffled. I, like you have watched countless films where the ghostly apparitions walk through walls and doors without resistance from solid matter. Solid matter however passing through solid matter is something very different indeed. East Drive was seemingly playing a game of 'catch me when you can.' Like the majority of unexplained activity the button incident only added to a never ending list of happenings which somehow chose the moment when no cameras were filming.

Twelve months have now passed since my innocent first visit to the semi-detached ex-council house in Pontefract. Little did I know on that spring day would my beliefs be changed forever. Ghosts, hauntings and apparitions interested me from an early age but for me these were things of story time and amusing television shows and movies. Fiction had turned into fact and I was now convinced the house was home to something beyond human understanding. Each visit yielded phenomena which we could not replicate or explain. What began as a simple visit armed with a digital camcorder had ended with an array of equipment needing two cases to transport. My previous books had cost me nothing financially to research other than time and flights to Bosnia. Researching The Black Monk however had proved heavy on the pocket; financially the investigation had cost me dearly. Intrigue and excitement however outweighed cost and for me the last twelve months have been a roller coaster ride which I feel proud to have taken. 30 East Drive had completely changed my own inner beliefs about the paranormal. Deep down I had always believed there was something but before now could never say I had documented evidence of spiritual activity.

Chapter Twelve
Putting Fred to Bed

My time at East Drive was sadly drawing to a close. Each and every visit to the property had been better than the last and there was never any occasion when we had come away empty handed.

The quest had begun with just the two of us embarking on an adventure we did not understand. Steve and I had stumbled into the most haunted property we could have imagined on our very first outing.

Terror tales of an evil monk had been fuelled by the recent film and I admit on our first visits I would not explore any room without the company of others. Allegedly the monk had dragged the daughter upstairs by her throat leaving red marks across her neck. We soon earned the joint nickname of 'two idiots and the monk' as others voiced concerns we could be placing ourselves into a danger zone we did not understand. After that first visit to the house we were hooked and waited anxiously for our next foray into the unknown.

Despite our inexperience enthusiasm took control. We quickly began to gather evidence of paranormal activity. Unfortunately we found the world of paranormal investigation full of jealousy and backbiting amongst various groups all claiming to have the best evidence to date. We were ready for the sceptics but in house bickering amongst believers was a new experience.

Caution now was the order of the day and we were careful now with anything we released even to the paranormal world of supposed believers. Many say the hauntings have long since gone and the Black Monk finally found the peace he so desperately needed.

The hauntings have not gone and never were focused around one entity. The house is open to many spirits including those of children. I went in the house with the hope of recording evidence 'Fred' was real and came out in utter disbelief.

'Fred' I feel never actually existed. The Pritchard family experienced poltergeist activity on a huge scale and I suspect by simply putting a name to something they could not understand made them feel more reassured and at ease with what they were experiencing.

Ridicule and suspicion followed the family and I suspect it was this which added to the flow of similar experiences from other residents of the sprawling estate to be kept away from the public gaze.

Despite eliminating the ghostly monk as being the main perpetrator at East Drive I do believe the house and ground have a close connection to the Cluniac Order. The land on two sides of the property were in fact farmed by monks from the nearby priory. Hand drawn maps name these areas as Flaghill and Bendle Hedge. Working the land by hand would have been an arduous task especially in the hot summer months. Cold, clean water would have offered a welcome respite from their toil and it makes sense the monks would have utilised the nearby well for refreshment and place of rest.

My own grandfather had such a well on his beloved allotment and my own fond childhood memories of taking in the ice cold water as I took shade from the scorching sun stay with me today. The monks would have associated the area around the well as that of being welcoming and safe. When the gateway had been opened it was fond memories which led the spirits to a place they remembered and loved from a life long gone.

Unfortunately I suspect other entities had sought out whatever gateway had been created. One in particular did not follow the peaceful dream of the Cluniac Order. During our time spent at East Drive it was this oppressive entity which gave us cause for concern. The foul odours would always mark its entrance and any positive feelings soon diminished. This was the active player in the house. A feeling of being unwelcome always followed. Batteries somehow drained instantly of power.

Untouched a static tripod mounted camera would lose focus or simply turn itself off. Motion detectors turned around to face nearby walls, rendering them useless. This was The Black Monk of Pontefract at play, the same entity guilty of causing havoc to the Pritchard family.

Anyone interested in fishing will know the deadly pike. This ferocious predator reigns supreme in our rivers and ponds and sends shockwaves of terror amongst all other species of fish. Whenever pike are absent from the immediate area the angler, with luck and skill will attract fish to their baited hook.

Underwater interest will provide regular hits and provide a day of happiness with tales of the one that got away. Unfortunately pike are also active and seek out areas wherever fish are in abundance and feeding. Suddenly the once active water becomes void of fish activity. No amount of coaching with fresh bait will entice a catch and momentarily the angler questions either his skills or the methods used. The pike has entered the area and fearing their safety all other fish have gone. Satisfied with a full belly the predator takes rest in the dark corners of the water. Suddenly the fish are back and the angler once again reels in the fish to fill the net.

This was 30 East Drive during my time there. Like the angler I would set out equipment in the faint hope of catching something I could not later replicate and dismiss. More often than not the results came in thick and fast. EVP's were recorded, K11 readings fluctuated and banging noises seemed to come from every unoccupied room. Suddenly all readings would cease and pungent odours made staying in the same room impossible. In my opinion this was the real cause of the historic haunting at East Drive. Whatever gateway had been opened gave access to something alien to the surrounding land and thrived on fear.

Fear was the feeding point and this had easily been found in the family. With each episode of activity the intensity would have increased. Mr Pritchard, I am reliably informed, wanted to turn his back on the house and move to another property. His wife however had a different view and refused to give in. Unfortunately as time passed Mr Pritchard died and the two children left to seek out their own lives leaving Mrs Pritchard alone. She continued to reside there until just a few years ago before moving into a nearby sheltered housing complex. It is apparent she kept things tightly guarded following the release of Colin Wilson's book 'Poltergeist' and no one to date has offered any evidence of further poltergeist activity during the remainder of her time at the property. Did the activity cease or had she simply learned to accept and live alongside whatever it was that shared the home she cherished. I had been informed Mrs Pritchard continued her time living mostly in the kitchen area in the company of her pet parrot. It seems she avoided spending time within the living room. Could this be the reason why the internal doors separating this room from the kitchen having a lock fitted?

Given my own time spent there I now suspect the former of the two. With the father and children gone the fear factor had been reduced starving the entity of the energy it craved. Why then after an almost forty year interval did activity in the house resume?

Mrs Pritchard finally sold the house to the film producer who was in the final stages of releasing the movie 'When the Lights Went Out.' Interest once again grew and crowds flocked to the house in the hope of taking a look inside. With the Pritchard family gone the interior was left void of anything other than carpets, wallpaper, fixtures and fittings. No stage was ever complete without the addition of props to set the scene.

The fear factor was again ignited with the film. When the cameras began rolling Mrs Pritchard remained in the house and a substitute location was used. By the time the cinemas were screening the story she had sold the property to the producer who now had sole rights to the house.

Interest once again grew and the Black Monk was reborn. Crowds waited impatiently outside and duly paid the entrance fee for a brief guided tour of the house they had just recently sat and ate popcorn whilst watching the family's plight on the big screen.

Fear was already instilled into the crowd and this would most certainly have been expanded once they were inside the house.

Gullibility is a dangerous state and can lead the unwary into a strong belief of something which may not be entirely true. If this was the case with East Drive then the fear factor would reoccur. With an appetite satisfied once again the gateway could be opened and the bridge separating the spirit world and ours was again open to traffic.

I believe, also, the newly installed furniture plays a part to the resurrection of activity within the house. The new owner had filled each room with second hand items probably acquired through local charity shops.

Charity shops offer low cost, good quality goods to a public in need of a bargain. Unfortunately the items can harbour a sense of sadness and loss. Bereavement can often lead to once happy homes being cleared in readiness for new occupants and a lot of furniture finds its way into the shops by this route.

In my opinion the furniture and fittings play some part in today's activity. There are many theories inanimate objects can be linked or attached to the deceased who treasured the item in life.

Modern technology also plays a part in the modern story of the Black Monk. Digital cameras and mobile phone capabilities offer the chance for immediate playback of images captured seconds before. There is no need to wait for the film to be processed in the dark room and it's all too easy for an excited individual to see something on screen and make an immediate assumption as to what they see. Once installed into their inner self belief it is often difficult to alter this. The face in the wallpaper and reflection in the mirror is now real and no amount of dissuasion or rationality will ever debunk what can easily be brushed away with logic. Once uploaded to social media with a description of what the image portrays a new audience of believers is created adding to the interest and belief.

History repeats itself and it is evident the use of the Ouija Board was once again introduced by some visitors to the house. Not only do I suspect the board being used by someone connected to the Pritchard family there was evidence it was still being used in the house.

This practice should never have happened at East Drive and I suspect it was used by those who did not fully understand the board's potential. Ouija is not the game it was intended to be when first introduced and it takes knowledge and expertise to close it down correctly once the session has ended.

The board had been the final segment to complete the circle and now the house had once again became open to paranormal activity. As the crowds continued the fear factor increased and the house in effect has become a feeding ground to any spirits capable of passing through the doorway.

The Black Monk of Pontefract it seems now had a new audience to perform to. Despite my findings, I continue to refer to the hauntings at East Drive as being that of the Black Monk. Perhaps this is the romantic within me, wishing to preserve the story of a man perhaps wrongly accused of a hideous crime which he may or may not have committed.

The monk is not in any way singular, but rather a collection of entities feeding on fear and weaknesses. The Pritchard's centred their beliefs on simply what they had believed. All activity was credited without question, to the long dead Cluniac murderer. Credit has to be given to the family's resilience and determination to remain in the house despite the horrors encountered. Recently I was asked during a BBC radio interview if I would personally live in the house. My answer was an emphatic, no. If only one entity was present then, perhaps, I would take the risk. Unfortunately, in my opinion, this is not the case. 30 East Drive is unpredictable, which can be likened to that of a dormant volcano. Thrill seekers visit, and continue to visit in the hope of glimpsing a malevolent force present. At this moment in time, any malevolent force is, I believe, in a state of hibernation. Just how many of these thrill seekers would take the ride to the summit knowing eruption was near and unpredictable, is open to debate?

The story had begun in innocence and we expected to simply investigate a well known local story. As with the Pritchard's all activity was credited without question to the long dead Cluniac murderer.

For me this would have been the end and would have made writing the book far easier than what it had been. Like my previous research in Bosnia I would not rest until I separated fact from fiction. Bosnia remains an old country of deep rooted secrets and scars and will never open up to the truth of what she knows. Unfortunately with the non-existence of accurate historical records I fear 30 East Drive will slowly be lost also forever.

'Fred' or Father Michael does frequent the house on a regular basis. He is not a rapist, paedophile or murderer but simply a man who worked the land and gave his life to a god he believed was the creator of everything. Whenever Father Michael or any other of the monks cross the gateway into our world then visitors to East Drive are in safe hands. The monks are simply visiting a place they held in high esteem during their earthly lives. They are once again taking refuge from their toil of tending the crops, enjoying respite the well offered from the overhead rays of a summer sun long since gone.

Brother Michael however is very different. He lived on the ground which is now 30 East Drive. Brother does not relate to a man of the cloth rather than that of being a sibling. The area was known as Gill Croft and much of the land was covered with fruit trees, in short an orchard. Michael it seems had a brother called Simon who unfortunately had a liking for young girls.

Five hundred years ago an orchard during the months of ripening would have been like a modern sweet shop to the young. This would have been a predator's paradise. Victims could be discarded with ease on the hillside and without modern day forms of investigation disappearances would go unrecorded.

Somehow Simon's day was over. A lynch mob probably descended on the croft and took the law (if indeed there was any) into their own hands. Unfortunately Brother Michael was home and the crowd may have assumed him to be the slayer of the local girls. Without trial he was dragged to the nearest tree and lynched. I believe the spectacle of a dying man struggling on the rope may have been too much for some of the audience to endure resulting in the rope being cut and Michael's dying body being deposited into the nearby well to finally drown. This may well have been a final warning to the occupants of Gill Croft that they were not welcome and the water source was now contaminated and rendered useless.

Without a water supply the croft would have become uninhabitable and, coupled with local hostility the family would have been forced to leave the area. What happened to them, and in particular to Simon, I have uncovered nothing. Earlier voice recordings indicate eight young girls could have been murdered.

Seven of these had been the target of a deranged sexual predator and the eighth may have been an innocent witness which the killer had to erase for the sake of self-preservation. Local speculation remains that each of the bodies were hidden within the depths of the well. This certainly is a myth. Simon relied on the water for his own survival and would not have endangered the commodity by making the water undrinkable. I suspect the answer may lie within the enclosed grounds of the croft. Pigs were a common animal and valuable source of farm produced meat. I fear the young bodies were simply fed to the animals removing all trace of their earthly existence.

My time at 30 East Drive finally ended. It had been a rollercoaster ride of adventure and learning. Fear had overcome me on many occasions but thankfully I survived the experience.
The house holds many mysteries which still need to be uncovered. Given a lack of accurate historic records I fear the true story will never be entirely uncovered. 'Don't Look Back in Anger' simply brings the story up to date.
'Fred' remains within the ground he knew and will he continue to walk his path. Simon the child killer is also present and it is he who is connected with evil and the dark side. Despite having no connection to the Cluniac Order it is Simon who became known as the Black Monk of Pontefract. Evil in life he remains unfortunately evil in death. His spirit has become the

notorious pike keeping the spirits of innocents at bay whenever his dark presence is felt.

Spirits of children are abundant within 30 East Drive and I suspect some of these may be unfortunate victims of the killer. Other spirits have no real connection to the house and simply make use of the doorway to cross over into the living world.

What is important to remember to anyone visiting the property is to show respect. They say behaviour breeds behaviour and this is not lost within the spirit realm. Enter the house with an open mind and never expect something which may never happen. You are merely a spectator and in no way control anything which may or may not happen.

I make one last reference to fishing as the book finally draws to a close. The angler at times will return with an empty net. This does not lessen his or her enthusiasm for the sport and in no way proves fish do not exist. Paranormal activity is like this. Accept what you catch and never dismiss anything, without doing your research, with an open mind.

The road had been a difficult one to manoeuvre from its very start to its final conclusion. We expected little and gained a lot. What seemed like a boyish adventure turned into almost an obsession as each visit gave us another fragment of the puzzle to piece together.

Today there are three main parties, each having their own personal beliefs about 30 East Drive. One side of the fence is occupied by non-believers who feel that perhaps once paranormal activity did in fact take place but in time this has long since gone. Spaces taken on the other side are filled with those who do believe activity prevails, albeit on a lower level. This belief is usually supported by visits and dismissing everything which can be rationally explained.

Then there are those who casually sit on the fence, interested in the story but casting their own beliefs on neither side. I began as a fence sitter. Intrigued and drawn to a story which was ingrained within my childhood recollections, fondly remembered in nostalgia. Comfort upon the fence came to a sudden end when I felt pushed onto the side of believer. Countless experiences and recorded phenomena I could not explain sealed the divide and now the fence is simply one sided. East Drive is a fascinating place and we have collected much evidence which we cannot simply answer with any rationale.

For me the journey has finally ended. It seemed I was in safe hands with 'Fred'. If indeed he was real then thankfully I was accepted as a friend and not his enemy.

I have met some fantastic people along the way and forged friendships I hope will continue into the future. For those who helped make the book a reality I salute you with never ending thanks. 30 East Drive has been a journey I could never have truly imagined.

Ingram Content Group UK Ltd.
Milton Keynes UK
UKHW021311130423
420112UK00024B/757